Björn Thorvald

the Norse Mythology Bible

6 BOOKS IN 1

Epic Tales of Myths of the Northern Lands.
Discover Gods and Goddesses, Origins and
Traditions, Viking Battles, Ancient Runes
and All the Values of Norse Paganism

! BONUS !

DIY Viking Crafts Guide

Discover and learn the ancient Viking art, build your favorite items of Norse culture with this simple and practical step-by-step guide!

Scan the Qr Code below to download your FREE bonus NOW!

TABLE OF CONTENTS

FOREWARD

Mythsarerooted deep, like the Yggdrasil Tree. They are a bedrock culture. There all etched a part of human history and spoken to kindle a fire to inspire. From the myth of The Roman Emperor, Nero fiddled while Rome burned, The Great Flood, The Trojan Horse and the conquest of Troy or The Divine Wind, which destroyed Mongol invasions of Japan. They communicate the human condition in morality tales and are passed on throughout generations. Understanding Norse Mythology is like slowly getting the drape removed from many fantasy writers throughout history. Their inspirations are crystal clear.

When one researches all there is about Northern mythology and what that entails, you see just how far-reaching it is within human history. This book takes a lot of research from Poetic Edda and Prose Edda. (Edda for Eddukvaeoi. Meaning: education). Where that info is from is fifty five vellum pages from the Icelandic book called the Codex Regius. It was discovered in 1643 and believed it was written in the 1270s. That ar-

chaic book with aged brittle pages, is Poetic Edda poems came from in 9th or 8th century. Scholar believe the Codex Regius is a copy of something written in the 1200, as theorized by the spelling of words. Since the eighties, that compendium book, chronicling the ancient battles and ancient gods in somewhat cryptic language, has resided in Iceland in the Árni Magnússon Institute for Icelandic Studies.

With Poetic Edda are a patchwork collection of 13th-century poems and stories put together by a historian named Snorri Sturluson. He was an Icelandic historian, poet, and politician—a bard of his times. He elected twice as law speaker of the Icelandic parliament and the foremost expert of the Old Religion. He was a member of the powerful Icelandic clan known as at the Sturlungar. According to Icelandic naming traditions, "Sturlulson' literally reflects who the author Snorri's father was. (He is Sturla's son) and is not an inherited last name. The architect recording these myths converted to Christianity during the times of Holy Roman Emperor Otto II of 973 to 983, He was one of the reasons why so many of the legends were preserved and encapsulated into this book. Before all of this was to be lost to hands of time by the gradual Christianization of Europe and Scandinavia, he put down the mythos into feathered pen and quill. Using his due diligence, he put forth stringent

research and compiled many of the stories and put them into two books called Poetic Edda and Prose Edda. Throughout this book, many excerpts are used in poetic form that crystallizes the imagery into the reader's mind.

Between the 8th and 12th centuries, was the bloody time when Christianity spread throughout Scandinavia. Aspects of Norse Paganism began to almost vanished like leprosy. Thus, this bard named Snorri Sturluson compiled these two books through a hodgepodge of sources, including the opening Völuspá to compile the cosmology and belief system and morality tales into one volume so it can stand hourglass of time. This is a Mammoth project, a synthesis of many sources, as big as the first frost giant, Ymir, who stomped out of the mountains embedded in ice.

As a frost-bitten Northerner myself, a student of history, this undertaking, I hope all my readers have an informative read and enjoy embarking and disseminating the adventures with Odin, Thor, Freya, and the always mischievous Loki, the aspirations of this book and that book by Snorri Sturluson, and this book here is to make the complex clockwork of these myths accessible for consumption and a pleasant reading experience and perhaps find inspiration in whatever they aspire to become

in this thing called life. Now get your dagmal porridge my fellow Vikings, and let's begin this adventure of mysticism and history.

Skåll!

Björn Thorvald

INTRODUCTION

Long, long, long ago, many Gods were venerated by the Vikings. For those ancient warriors with their horns and their blades, they worshipped are two pantheons of Gods. The Æsir and the Vanir. There are many deities to deify, like The God Of Thunder by the name of Thor, but there are a treasure trove of Gods and goddesses, Giants and giantess that many people who are new to the world of Norse Mythology don't know about that are fascinating mythological beings with impactful stories.

The Old Norse Religion has its genesis during the Iron Age. And if you aren't a scholar of history, that would be around the year one-thousand two-hundred before that carpenter named Christ. But unlike that certain book called the Bible, this religion was communicated among practicers in conversations, there wasn't a defining book, one codified text, which one could find answers from. The known archaeologist Anders Andrén would call the religion a, "cultural patchwork." This means it's

rooted in many Pre-Old Norse Religions like Nordic Bronze Age with a solar belief system or early Germanic Iron Age Religions. Old Norse belief system is of non-doctrinal community religion. Which means, it's not exactly telling you how to govern your life but rather give you mythology and stories that can inspire you and learn from. Perhaps, in finding some solace in believing in things like the Alfather.

That book aspired to take the reader on a wondrous journey through the fascinating realm of North mythology and unlocking its tantalizing mysteries of it. If the gamut of Greek mythology is Zeus's endless love affairs of things of all sorts. Then the gamut of Norse mythology is the sabotaging pranks of Loki. Through these pages there is double-crossing Gods known (or Quadruple Crossing, for that matter), monstrous creatures, anthropomorphized animals, and Twilight of Gods in Ragnarök with heroic battles all encapsulated in morality tales. Many of these stories transcend time because they are timeless stories of human nature. Now welcome my weary travelers; you're in an informative book exploring the furthest regents of the depths of Old Norse Mythology. One of the more insightful things one takes away from learning about Norse Mythology: etymology. Study of the roots of words and changes through the spans of

millennia For instance, the word Wednesday came from the father of all fathers himself, Odin.

Within these pages these berserker people, known as the Vikings once thought of Norris mythology like many people see Christianity. It was a time-tested religion for Norse people and the Scandinavians of a bygone time. Just as much many worshipped a carpenter named Jesus, Moses, Noah, Adam and Eve and the insidious Judas. The Nordic People worshipped in a Polytheism fashioned, meaning multiple deities. In sharp contrast from Christianity, where there is Monotheism—one God. A singular deity. One would make an educated guess that having so many different deities, increasing the head-spinning complexity of it, one was the catalyst for the religion to dying out the bubonic plague. It's also less clear cut that Christianity is less black and white of good and evil and dogmatic. Perhaps more reminiscent to real life there is a key element of grey and where characters and places are wholly ambiguous and not clearly defined as nefarious or angelic. For instance, in the Old Norse version of Hell, also known as Helheim, it is a place where many it's not exactly the burning subterranean furnace for the villainous. But Hell, it is an afterlife where some people they went there of old age and her less remarkable lives of com-

mon everyday folk. For instance, this author may go to hell just for writing this book by that logic. It is not a place of fire and brimstone which are staples of Christian imagery.

On the flipped, there is heaven. The place with old Norse Mythology, or Old Norse religion that would be signifies heaven is Valhalla and Fólkvangr would you be covered in detail in this book. Another thing about the Old Norse Religion, there is no priesthood. The cultic actives were commenced by common people of the religion. No professional was trying to proselytize you into the belief of a Thunder God, not me. All in all, it's a complex clockwork of stories dealing with mysticism, magic, animism and shamanism and does not derive from one single book... or one single person to worship like Christ.

As you can see, there is sharp contrast between Christianity and Old Norse Religion, making the topic a novice quite compelling to learn. Through there is a oodles of stuff here to cover. Old Norse Religion, One of the reasons why Old Norse Religion is kind of muddled and contradictory: it was told in the spoken world through people. There is no Bible to to get the precise meaning of folklore tales and, but rather, it was spoken to by Vikings, Scandinavians and then sometimes carved

NORSE MYTHOLOGY

1.1 THE DAWN OF CREATION

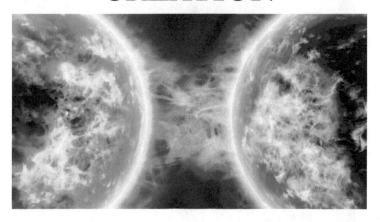

O nce there was one oblivion known as **Ginnungagap** (JINN-NUN-A-GAP). It is a vast emptiness in the cosmos of nothingness and everything is derived from in all creation. Throughout Norse Legends, it would be best described as the veil of darkness with two regions in chaos with one another. Within this spacetime of near

nothingness, there were these two areas: the scorching infernos of Muspelheim and, on the other by icy encrusted Niflheim of the frost-bitten South. Within the regions of, they began to conflict the northern inferno of Muspelheim started to melt the permafrost in the ice of Niflheim. Like a chain reaction, all life came froth into fruition like a spring over the entire universe. Written in the year 961, the Icelandic poem Völuspá (Vol-Us-Spa) described Ginnungagap as,

THAT WAS THE AGE WHEN NOTHING WAS,

THERE WAS NO SAND, NOR SEA, NOR COOL WAVES,

NO EARTH NOR SKY NOR GRASS THERE,

ONLY GINNUNGAGAP

Within the Bible, there is the opening of Genesis, and within science, there is a thing called The Big Bang. Within Norse Mythology, this would be the spitting image of that universe-expanding event that shook the galaxy to its core and

the clockworks of the commencement of all creation.

THERE WAS IN TIMES OF OLD,

WHERE YMIR DWELT,

NOR SAND NOR SEA,

NOR GELID WAVES;

EARTH EXISTED NOT,

NOR HEAVEN ABOVE,

'TWAS A CHAOTIC CHASM,

AND GRASS NOWHERE.

A monstrous thing came forth from the melting of these two hemispheres. Out of this cosmogenetic process, there were changes like a melting pot. The snow trench regions entombed in ice trampled the first primordial giant named **Ymir** (Ee-Mir). A monstrous thing and the progenitor of the giants known as the

Yötnar (*Yu-mir*), first giant and the ancestor to all giants in the galaxy. He also was the first Jötunn, the supernatural entity that juxtaposed with the Gods that would clash with them. Within Norse mythology, it is recorded that this horned titan Ymir lived in the icy regions of worlds unknown in Niflheim. There was no living thing of any kind that drew breath before Ymir. That same poem Völuspá (From the Poetic Edda) described him as, Another being materialized came out of the glaciers. That comic being would be known as **Auðumbla**. (A Doone-ya), cow. Though one learns this was not any lowly cow but a super being cut from the same cloth as the aforementioned, for when this cow came forth from eternal hibernation. Ymir fed off this cow, and then, within the change of temperature, he started to sweat when he slept.

FROM YMIR'S FLESH

THE EARTH WAS FORMED,

AND FROM HIS BONES THE HILLS,

THE HEAVEN FROM THE SKULL

OF THAT ICE-COLD GIANT,

AND FROM HIS BLOOD THE SEA.

This primeval cow in 13th-century poem is known as Völuspá:

From there, the inconceivable cow Auðumbla licked ice tufts known as a salty rime and ice blocks. The first living beings materialized. Over the course of three days in this merciless cold, the cow the ice licked the salty ice day in and day out. From his tongue on salty ice, out of that came forth some hairs. Then upon the second day an angelic head and third a body came forth. Finally, out of that primordial frost came the first

Norse God known as **Búri**, (bor-ee). It was said that Æsir deity and was the progenitor of All Gods. They are known as upper-echelon Gods in Norse Mythology. It was said the countenance of face was handsome as he thawed in the entombed ice. Three god's came from this ancient thawing ice.

He also was the First Norse God and married **Hárm**.

Out of Ymir's skin came a giantess **Bestla** and another Æsi god named Borr.

In this dawn of creation, they had three sons, **Odin**, the Father of All. This particular god is one of the most revered Gods in Norse Mythology. He has the classic long of long beard and he also has an association with wisdom. He was also a propagator of a magic called Seiðr (or Seid), a feminine magic from the Goddess Freyja. Odin was not the strongest by way of might of all the Æsir Gods, but he was the most powerful in the pantheon. For his wisdom and sight was as deep as oceans. All throughout the Viking history and Paganism, the god sometimes known as Woudan, was the most worshipped, excluding Thor. The Word "Wednesday" is also derived from his Old Dutch name as, Wuodan, as in Wuodan's Day. He had two lesser-known brothers, **Vili** and **Vé**. All of the gods lived in these freshly burned regions of the galaxy as, with colossal horned ice giant

Ymir lurking near. It is then recorded in various Eddeic poems throughout the iron age that Odin and his brothers conquered the ice giant Ymir. Within the Norse pantheon, it is documented that the three brothers slew the mountain-sized behemoth by tearing him to pieces, and from that, the three dragged the dead frost giant to the very center of Ginnungagap. It's as this Odin and his brothers devised the world.

That same Eddic poem described this event as,

THEY TOOK YMIR AND TRANSPORTED HIM TO THE MIDDLE OF GINNUNGAGAP,

AND OUT OF HIM MADE THE EARTH, OUT OF HIS BLOOD THE SEA AND THE LAKES.

THE EARTH WAS MADE OF THE FLESH AND THE ROCKS OF THE BONES, STONE,

AND SCREE THEY MADE OUT OF THE TEETH AND MOLARS AND OF THE BONES THAT HAD BEEN BROKEN.

After The Giant Amir's death, the brothers started the world as we know it. Ocean came from the spilled blood and furtive lands from bones and flesh. From the frost giant's skill, they made the sky. From that came Gods and Giants and all creation and all nine realms of the world were created nine extradimensional places.

Alfheim, The domain of the Light Elves.   The elves are described to be as radient like the son.

Asgard, The place of Odin, Thor and the chief temple of the Aesir Gods

Jötunheim, The land of the giants.   Odin and Thor would venture on quests there.

Midgard, an earthy Earth place where humans reside.

Muspelheim, The domain of inferno and fire giants. Within the flames it is ruled by the Fire Giant Surtr. It is one of the early worlds that began the creation of the nine realms.

Nidavellir/Svartalfheim, The place of the Elves. This one is a bit of a mysterious and schollars aren't sure if run by Elves or Black Elves. There is a subterranean era called Niðavellir.

Niflheim/Niflheim, The domain of everlasting cold that placed into the opening cosmetology.

Vanaheim, The domain of the Vanir Gods, the most notable being the brothers and sisters of Freyja and Freyr. Njord is the ruler of the realm.

Helheim, The House of Hel, the underworld. Not a place of fire but rather people who died of old age. It is surrounded by a river known as **Gjöll** that no soul can leave. That is a uncrossing river that distinguishes the living from the dead.

All of these realms connected to one thing:

Yggdrasill (Yeg-Dra-Sill), The "Tree Of The World." This tree is directly below the Helheim. It connects all the realms together in an energy field. From Asgard, Alfheim, to Midgard, and onward, their all interconnected through this world tree. It is a scared cosmic tree and references throughout these Iron Age fables of good, evil.   One of the more nefarious nature, living beneath it is a dragon that crawls that the roots named **Nidhoggor Níðhöggr.** He devours the corpses of evildoers in a place **Náströnd** (Nid-hog-gr), in afterlife place in **Niflheim.**

After this creation of all things in the cataclysmic event

of fire and ice and blood, Amir's flesh had tiny larvae which originated from the dwarfs and the elves in their dwelling in Alfheim. (Elf-Heim) Then came the Earthy place **Midgard.** Beowulf is an an Old English epic poem written in the 8th century. It is considered one of the most vital pieces of writing in all of English literature. Within it Midgard was referred to as Middangeard. Throughout this book many of the names have other names as these stories were mostly transferred word of mouth. Midgard uninhabited kingdom that needed people to fill fertile lands. It was a desolate land that that needed life.

The Æsir God's divine solution: From the two trunks on the edge of the ocean's beach, they decided that these logs would create mankind. From this came the first porto-humans by the name of **ASK** and **EMBLA** (*Ask* and *Em-Bla*). Thereafter, the Alfather Odin gave them lifeblood, and their eyes sprung open and they drew their first breath. For Villa, he gave intelligence and Vey gave them eyes, ears and mouths. For this, Odin is known as "The father of all".

Within this early phase of cosmic creation, the brothers then created the Place of **ASGARD,** the dwelling of Æsir Gods. It was gold encrusted within both the exterior and interior and connected to the other twelve realms by a rainbow bridge known

as the **Bilröst Bridge.** Many of these fragmented Kingdoms that no mortal men knew of. As the other Gods in the principal pantheon, the architects of creation, the Aeir Gods dwelled in the palace with its stately halls. Each of the Æsir Gods had their own lofty palace. Odin's home, known as Valhalla he, dwelled in this early phase of time. Within the Old Norse tongue, Valhalla translated to *Hall of the Slain.* A heavenly place where only Gods and souls that die in dignified and courageous fashion dwelled. A dreamlike palace with huge and decadent golden halls. Within its rafters were warrior's shields and ominously pointed spears. Within this place were banquets as the Gods feasted and waited for their next thing to partake in. Within this place, the father of all waited. For Odin, he wanted to reach his furthest potential of wisdom.

1.2 THE ALFATHER'S LOST EYE

T hefather of all, Odin is the preeminent God known throughout northern Europe and the world. He was known by various names and monikers throughout the Iron Age. Chief among them, an Old English, he was known Wōden in Old

Saxon as Uuôden. In Old Dutch, he was known as Wuodan. Throughout history and the globe, Odin is known to have 170 names and allies in human history. Besides his offspring, the hammer-welding Thunder God Thor, he was the benchmark for the most famous Norse Pegan God of them all. As a matter of fact, throughout Europe, there is places named after him, such as Odense, one of the largest cities in Denmark. Odin would have two ravens known as Huginn for thought and then Muninn for memory. Also worthy of mention, he would have an eight-legged horse named Sleipnir. The Lord of the Æsir Gods would go on to be a central figure in Ragnarök, the Twilight of The Gods.

He would go on to marry a goddess named **Frigg** - (or *Frigga*). She was a member of the opposing deity of Gods, known as the **Vanir.** She would be known for her lustrous long hair and was the matriarch of the Æsir pantheon upon marriage. One other astonishing thing known about her, is the word Friday is derived from her name. The Goddess Frigg could see what could happen to everyone and everything. She even foresaw the end of everything with Ragnarök. She had the power of knowledge and foreknowledge and prophecy, which

would lead to the foreboding prophecy of the death of her own child, **Baldr** - The beloved son of Odin. Also, the half brothers of thundered known as Thor. After a prophecy came of his demise, she asked for anybody to swear an oath to never hurt her son from the bloodlust of murder.

Within present Day Earthly Norway, there is a place known as **Jötunheim**, named after the home of the giants. A place of misted mountains region of the world where thousands of stories to be told within the Norse Cannon. Throughout this real-life place, it is consumed with the folklore of myths that are the bedrock of Norse Mythology. That is the location where the next segment of this book will delve into, and we learn one greatest myths about him: how Oden lost his eye when he sought counsel on the nature of ascertaining more wisdom.

Thereupon, the Father of All sat within his thrones of Valhalla. He knew he did not know all there is to know of creation. Odin's true gift was his thirst for knowledge of all affairs. So much so that he had two ravens named **Hugin** and **Munin**. The two black birds gave Odin tidings of the world. For he wanted gain more from and learn more there is to learn and sought council. So within the twilight hours, he left his palace of perfect twinkling gold and headed through the nightfall

dressed as a wonderer. He had a wide-brimmed hat and grey cloak and keen eyes for knowledge. But as Odin trekked through forests through arduous hours through heaths and hilltops. For many a day, he went onward and spearheaded through the countryside in a noble quest for knowledge. He was much-traveled and weary of walking onward, and then he came upon a realm down as **Jötunheim** (*Yotten-hime*). Place is known for its colossal giants and all other nemesis of the Gods. Within this place, Odin is near a Well of Knowledge or Mímisbrunnr. The waters of the well-fed ash tree of **Yggdrasil.** It was a secret tree that fed knowledge with its deep roots and was humongous in size and was the biggest and the fairest of all trees. Near it, there was a well where one could attain more wisdom of the world. **Mímisbrunnr** (Which in Old Norse translated to "Mímir's Well). It was near it the world-weary God came upon his own uncle, the gatekeeper of the enchanted well. Standing flatfooted before the mystical well was an ancient deity named **Mímir.** *(My-Mere). An Æsir* god is known to be the wise one of them all and a water spirit in the same token of breath.

Odin looked upon Mimir with world-weary eyes as he saw him use his horn, the Gjallarhorn, (*Gall-a-Horn*), to drink

the water from the well. Whenever he consumed this divine water, his understanding of the world would expand. Through many days Odin traveled to acquire some of this and wanted to bargain with fellow blood relatives Æsir God.

Odin himself felt unworthy of the title of Lord of the Gods if he did not, in the same token of breath, have more knowledge there is to know. He wanted an in-depth study of everything he did not know with a mind thirsty for understanding. So as he raised his wide-brim hat and his sharp sights drew upon his fellow God, he asked a noble question. As their eyes converged near the well, Odin asked to drink some of that water of knowledge and wanted to reach True Wisdom.

"My fellow kinsmen of the Æsir Pantheon, this is your Nephew Odin. I ask only that I can have a drink from your sacred well?"

Near his sacred well, "Mímir' said,

«Nay, the price of drinking from this well is high." Then he said, "The Price is your eye. I want you to pluck your eye out and throw it into the well and so you can drink from it."

So near that tree of Yggdrasil was an enchanted stone well **Mímisbrunnr (***Mímir's Well*****)** Odin did the unthinkable: he raised his hand to his face and twisted his fingers around his

eyeball. The agony, the pain went through him and he gripped his eyeball. It was then Odin plucked his eye out as the blood gushed and throughout the land of the giants, Jötunheim and then through the universe, his yell was heard like a thunderclap.

Odin placed his eye into Mímir's Well and floated there in the blood of water. Mímir nodded with approval of his sacrifice of his own half-sight. Then offered him a horn with water from his well and drank everything at once. As Lord of the Gods drank that lifeblood of knowledge from that well, he acquired the wisdom and his eye was replaced with a ghastly scar which sometimes glowed like coal laced with fire. At this time, the Father of All, Odin was known as the "One-Eye" or the one with the "Flaming Eye." With only one eye, he could see better than with both as he acquired the limitless power of knowledge that was more mighty than his single globe of sight. With the enlightenment from that water, his thirst for wisdom was settled. Under the cloak of nightfall, with the moonshining downward in his wide-brim hat, Odin and one missing eye but a mind full of wisdom that was quenched, throughout the Old Religion, Odin would go to another level more equally severe as that to acquire knowledge. It was written that from that divine world tree, **Yggdrasil**, he would hang himself for nine

nights. His rivets of blood were gushing down his cloak from a self-inflicted spear wound. He remained famous, fasting for nine gut-wrenching days of torment. It was then an epiphany, runes were revealed at the tree's roots. From this harrowing moment of self-sacrifice interment, he would learn about the first incarnation of the mystical things like cryptic letters. These would be called Elder Futharks, the genesis of runes and their enchanted properties to channel lore.

During the legendary Æsir–Vanir War, which isn't written about in great detail. But one learns of the face of the aforementioned Mímir. In the poem Völuspá there are lines about a certain female sorceress figure named Gullveig. Once again, the similar Iron Age source of poetry is the riddling mystery for this.

SHE REMEMBERS THE WAR, THE FIRST IN THE WORLD,
WHEN THEY STABBED AT GOLD-DRAUGHT WITH MANY SPEARS,
AND IN THE HALL OF THE HIGH ONE [ODIN] THEY BURNED HER BODY,
THREE TIMES THEY BURNED THE ONE THRICE-BORN,
OFTEN, OVER AGAIN; YET SHE LIVES STILL.

THEY CALLED HER BRIGHTNESS WHEN SHE CAME TO THEIR HOMES,
A WITCH WHO COULD FORETELL; SHE KNEW THE SKILL OF WANDS,
SHE MADE MAGIC WHERE SHE COULD, SHE MADE MAGIC IN A TRANCE;
SHE WAS ALWAYS A DELIGHT TO A WICKED WOMAN.

In it written in that would be found by the Aesir Gods and burned three times and upon her their time, she would be reborn as **Heiðr**. There is scholar debate if this Gullveig is shrouded figure the goddess Freyja of the Vanir. This torching of this woman, and then her Christlike resurrection what was the catalyst for the immortals battle for the ages. The Æsir–Vanir War was first war.

It would be then they would have a standstill and then a truce and then one learns about the fate of the prophetic figure Mimir. It would be said that after the battle of the two tribes, they would unify into one. It is up for scholarly debate on what transpired within the war as these legends were only spoken word of mouth, and many of the various codexes are cryptic, brief, and enshrouded in the mystery of millennia of time. But in more unsettling revelation, Mimir would his head severed in the Æsir–Vanir War. Odin later would embalm the served head of Mimir with enchanted herbs and kept him alive. He would be resurrected. It was told that in Pagan Lore, the All-Father held the deities' head. It would sprout alive and give him tidings of other countries of all nine realms.

Odin would be the most revered of all the Gods. For his sacrifice at Mímir's Well, he would have many monikers from

this gruesome myth. Chief of them would be "One-eyed" and the "One with the Flaming-Eye."

1.3 THE ORIGIN OF THOR'S HAMMER

I nthe palace of Asgard, the God of Thunder and the Son of Odin, Thor, was born. Throughout Norse Paganism Beliefs, he is one of the real staple figures of it but sides Oden and Loki.

This book Chronicle some of the real hallmark moments of his life which is a bedrock of overall Pagan mythos. Thor had a Son by name **Thjalfe**, and also daughter by the name **Roskva** and a lovely wife named **Sif** (SEFF) who is involved in one for the more outlandish myths in this whole book. She is attested to within the Poetic and Prose Edda compilation of stories, and she is known for to her ties to the earth and her long golden locks down to her back. The Thunder God Thor is described as having hair fairer than gold and, like Odin, has many different names he went by. He lived in a house called Bilskirnir in Asgard with five hundred and forty rooms and had a Belt called the Megingjarder. He is mentioned in many 13th-century poems, including the most well-known one, Völuspá, one of the primary resources for Norse Legends. That poem goes back to the 10th century before the Christianization of Iceland.

The poem of the Poetic Edda, a short collection of anonymously penned myths compiled by 13th-century historians. It is 65 short stanzas and also goes by the name of Sæmundar Edda. One of the key attributes of Thor is his Hammer which goes by the name of Mjölnir. Thor and his Hammer is a bedrock of Anglo-Saxon culture. How the Thunder God came upon that chapter will explore. In this story, Thor is a very young man and

has never acquired his Hammer.

The story goes as when Thor lies in bed in his home Bilskirnir in Asgard. One would imagine, the sun arrows were shining through the drapes with his long haired wife Sif beside him. But as Thor's eyes began to focus on the woman beside him, he find a stark revelation. The Thunder God was thunderstruck when he noticed that he woke up with a witch in his bed. A crone, maybe. Thor screamed and was heard through the Kingdom to and fro and echoed through the misty mountaintops and the fertile purple valleys.

As he lay in bed, and was horrified at who this woman was who laid bedside. Then the Norse God invested further into who this woman was and lo and behold, it was his wife with her golden locks amiss. Her head shone, and her head was bald like a marble banister. As Thor discovered more about what just happened through the halls of Asgard, his beloved wife's hair was sheared off like it was wool. Like a puzzle put together, he slowly learns that Uncle Odin's Brother, **Loki** (*Loak-ee*), a tricker Demigod is the culprit of the dastardly act. Loki, sometimes anglicized as **Loke is** a central figure of all of Norse Mythology. If the Bible head Judas for a betrayal, and the Greeks had Prometheus for betrayal, Norse Mythology has Loki

for betrayal. He is described as being fare faced, even beautiful even, but with a wicked, conniving, double-crossing, black heart of the corruptible seed. He son of giant **Fárbaut.** He also is a **Jötunn**, (Yo-din) (or normal spelling **Jötun**). He would go on to have terrible monsters with children they would play into Ragnarök, who will be referred to later. To summarize who Loki is, he negative being and sharply contrast the Æsir God's that Thor is. Though his father was of giant blood, he was a member of the elite tribe of Gods known as the Æsir. One of the more ironic things about Pagan mythology: the Gods frequently regained trust to Loki repeatedly---which is a bit puzzling to this author.

As we delve back into the myth God of Thunder was in Asgard, he laid in bed and was horrified by the bold woman. Thor concluded the mischievous God did something with his wife's hair.

With rage in his eyes and he did not have his Hammer yet, the Thunder God told Loki, "*If you do not give my wife to regain her elegant locks of hair, I will crush your skull with my first.*" As Thor desired to wring the God's neck and Loki knew he could be banished from the Kingdom for all eternity if he does not follow the Alfather, Odin's own son's command.

His, he dispatched the tricker God, Loki, to the Dwarf lands of **Spartaoheim** (other names: **Svartalfheim**). This is one of the nine realms in Norse Mythology that came into fruition and the dawn of creation.

The mischievous Loki and keen insight and knowledge of their skills at the craftsmanship and divine use of magic. Loki knew of the Ivaldi Dwarfs who are adept a fashioning a range of things, notwithstanding, the Skíðblaðnir, the flying ship. This vessel has one of the more supernatural things in the mythological pantheon, the ship can be folded up into a cloth, according to Prose Edda. So as Loki spearheaded toward the Kingdom of the dwarfs, a trial was commenced to see who could devise the greatest gifts for the Æsir Gods in Asgard.

Brokkr (Brock) and **Eitri** (Eat-tree) said the sons of **Ivaldi** (Ee-Val-Dee) do not have the chance to be the best artisans in Spartaoheim like the aforementioned Sons of Ivaldi. Loki asked for the brothers Brokkr and Eiti to construe ***Three Divine Gifts for the Gods.***

First and foremost, the golden hair of Thor's wife Sif. He wanted a healthy good-hearted competition between the two brothers, the sons of Ivaldi. However, they did not want to compete in the task. Loki but one of the more audacious things

that he requested, the perpetual mischievous God bet his own head on their failure. Though, he knew they were better than the Sons of Ivaldi.

In the darkness of the night, he traveled back on the rainbow bridge known as the Bilröst. He went back to Thor and told him about the competition and the clash of two families of Dwarfs. The Gods of Asgard, Odin, Thor, and Frey would judge and bequeath Loki's head with an iron blade.

"I would rather keep my head in this game of chance. I'm too handsome to get my head loped off like this." Loki murmured under his breath.

Loki saw the pair was doing something extraordinary and had to stop it to save his head. Brokkr and Eitri made two great gifts but made known also made the most astonishing gift Thor had ever seen of divine craftsmanship. It would be the signature weapon of the Thunder God.

It was a tool that the dwarfish smiths kept in their ford at a perfect temperature, not a degree more or less, in order perfect indestructible nature and featherweight so it could be tossed freewill and return reminiscent to a boomerang. Within the fiery furnaces of Spartaoheim Brokkr pumped the bellows with dwarfish precision skill. At last, out of that furnace was a divine

weapon. There was also a tool for the ages. That would be a Hammer known thought out Germanic Paganism as Mjölnir (*Me-or-near*). Within the Vafþrúðnismál, Benjamin Thorpe's 1866 translation: a scholar would translate the poem that after the Twilight of the Gods of Ragnarök, Thor's son would use the Hammer Mjölnir made by Dwarven blacksmiths in the subterranean Niðavellir.

As the powerful nature of the weapon was being tempered in the furnaces, Loki heard of the hammer being devised. He heard whispers of the unbeatable craftsmanship and saw visions of his own head hacks off. For within this kingdom's halls, the rogue God needed to thwart this precision craftsmanship to save his own head. Loki did what he did best to change the odds in his favor through his sickness and cunningness, for this god was had more skills than just pranks and treacherous wit. Loki, the son of Fárbauti and Laufey was also a renowned shapeshifter. Within Norse Mythology, he was endowed with the process known as **Hamrammr** or Eigi-Hamr (Hamir means the outer skin of a being.)

Within the twilight of the night, Loki used his skills of Hamrammr metamorphosis himself into a hematogenous

mosquito. As Loki in mosquito flew towards a fiery furnaces as the hammer was being sculpted by fire and dwarfish might, he stung Brokkr's hand.

"*Ouch,*" The dwarf said in a whisper. But was undeterred and continued creating his greatest creation for Thor. Then sting in the neck and there was little reaction. As Loki flew through the hair, he was hellbent on foiling the creation of the divine instrument known as Mjölnir. Then his stung the dwarf's eye and Brokkr belted a horrifying scream. Thus, fixed her hair and made a too-short hammer from a broken handle.

The Sons of Ivaldi presented the gifts for the competition. Golden hair for Sif for her bald head. Then Odin was gifted a **Gungnir, the spear,** beautiful and capable of piercing anything that would be later used in the climatic events of the end of the god's world at Ragnarök. Also, the supernatural weapon of the Alfather God's spear had the ability to have any oath made under the spear would be unbreakable.

One of the more humorous things the dwarfs fashioned would be given a boat that could be folded and fit into a pocket. This would be given to **Freyr,** or in anglicized spelling **Frey.** The ruler of the elves. He was the two most worshipped of all Vanir deities. The brother of Freyja and son of NJörd, Freyr was a

peaceful farmer and Vanir gods. He is shown as a big brawny man with his pet boar **Gullinborsti**. He is said to also ride a chariot drawn by giant boars.

Loki was euphoric about the gifts, he made to save his head from being loped off. The sons of Ivaldi, Brokkr and Eitri were asked to make three gifts for the god. Then Brokkr and Eitri presented their gift, Eitri had a puffy eye still. He gave bracelets of Draupnir to Odin. They also gave him a magical ring known as "**Draupnir.**" A material where new bracelets would fall from it like "drops." Frey was given a huge bore with golden fur would could be mounted and fly and the shine drew the darkness away from it like a torch in a catacombs. Then the last one, Thor, was given a **mighty hammer, MJölnir.** It was too short but still very powerful and unbreakable. A weapon that would make him The enthroned figure in Scandinavian history as one of the most worshiped Gods in the North mythology pantheon. The Gods deemed the mighty MJölnir hammer the best. Ultimately, Loki's plan of deception failed. It would not be his last game of trickery. But he would beg for his head and thought quickly. The machinations of his insidious mine were working. Loki was pondering of a way not to meet certain death.

Loki said, "You can sever my head as long as you do not damage

a single piece of my neck. The agreement says you can only have my head." Odin, "If people paid more attention to the words used, they would never negotiate with the cunning Loki, the trickster God." Brokkr sowed his mouth so he could never deceive anybody again. The Gods were euphoric about their divine and supernatural prizes and that Brokkr and Eitri won the contest for the ages.

Ultimately, the mischievous god Loki saved his head and Thor became the hammer-welding god. The Mjölnir, Thor'a hammer, would be worn as a Pendant during the age of the Vikings throughout Scandinavia. It is from his iconic divine instrument and is so revered by people that Thursday got its name from Thor's Day. He, like the other Gods were not immortal. For they all needed youth apples from the Goddness **Iðunn** (or Idun) regularly to remain youthful. In ripe fields, she would be the guardian of this life giving fruit for Gods. In the halls of Asgard, one could imagine the God Of Thunder munching on a life giving apple while he washes down some good ale.

1.4 THE WALL OF ASGARD

Withinthecelestial stronghold known as Asgard, Thor would protect it with all his vigor with his new hammer. Asgard was in many ways similar to the Greek's Heavenly Mount Olympus. The chief citadel of the god in the Æsir pantheon. It is described as a piece of land that levitates in space with gravity. It is the preeminent dwelling of the Norse Gods.

Through the summer and the frost, Thor would defend the heathen God's Kingdom with newfound ability and untampered power in the dwarf's tool. Chief among Æsir God's enemies that could attack was lumbering through the front giants and also one known as the **Surtur**, the fire demon who would come into to play with the end of the Gods, at Ragnarök. Within the e Poetic Edda, a collection of Icelandic poems put tether in a patchwork in the 13th century, Thor's hammer would be attested to. But

within the forest of Asgard, he would practice it and weld it with a mighty as it would be summoned under his command and returned to him under his own free will in the air.

The Destroyer of giants himself, Thor, left Asgard and this vulnerable. The gods heard tidings from others that danger was on the horizon. The Æsir Almighties held Council and agreed that needed fortification with a massive impregnable wall to encircle the Supreme Being's ornamented city. It was an opulent palace but in the same token of breath, defenseless of bombardment by forces. The Asgards needed to thwart it. They wanted a wall that would be devised in order to protect the Kingdom from the incursion of a rang of giants who could be lurking beyond the city. A war had unfolded that destroyed the wall around the most renowned Norse city of the Æsir God Tribe. Trampling in through the gates was a mysterious **Jötunn Builder. A** Which is Scandinavian myths Jötunn trolls. A being that something that contracted the more stately Æsir God's in their psychology. Jötunn Builder with his mare named **Svadilfari** and a cloak. With the legends little is inscribed about who exactly this Giant Mason, he is nameless. Through the gateway he came into the God's Palace lumbering through the gates on his high horse. One thing that is a theorized and foretold that he most likely

was of giant blood due to the inhuman audacity of his proposal. His bargain was to rebuild and refortify the wall to protect it from an onslaught of giants. His time frame to finish was in a inhuman three seasons.

As he approached the Gods with his offer, he also declared fearlessly what he coveted in female forms as token for his skillfulness. For the Gods were dismayed to find out he wanted in exchange was to marry the goddess known as **Freyja.** She was known for her divine beauty and also a prophet's ability like a seer. Other things slightly more otherworldly the Giants Manson wanted were the sun and moon. The Æsir Gods all collectively refused these requests and laughter at the Giant Mason's otherworldly proposal. But Loki as this moment, saw an opportunity to exploit to fortify vulnerable Asgard and bargain. He suggested he can't finish the wall in the precise time of three seasons, without any help but for his horse **Svadilfari**, and then he gets nothing in change for his deeds.

The Jötunn Builder and the other Gods of Asgard liked the proposal. However, very reluctantly. The Jötunn, skilled with masonry, started the fortification of surrounding ramparts around the city. The construction of the wall commenced and the Builder brought stones from the furthest-reaching quarries

to construct it. He would build the wall precisely and stack each block meticulously with lightning-fast speed. Through this process and as the months dragged on, the spring sprouted and the scorching summer came. Odin saw that Loki's scheme was on the threshold of failure. The Jötunn Builder was on the precipice of finishing the fortification with the aid of his horse Svadilfari. The rising wall was nearly totally encircling them. The God's were astounded at the rate of speed at which the mason builder could engineer this rampart. The Æsir God's went to Loki and told them he would meet his end unless they solved this problem.

It was within the time when the scheming and dealing Loki was none too pleased. Thus, he thought of ways to sabotage the Jötunn Builder to foil, a miraculous and far-reaching barrier. On the final minute, on the final day of the wall's completion, the Jötunn Builder was on the verge of placing the last block.

Loki worried about his fate.

He decided to use his skill with Hamrammr, shapeshifting into a mare, a female horse. As the Mason Giant and his horse Svadilfari spearheaded into a snowy forest, the Giant's horse saw the mare and bolted after it. This mare was Loki in disguise and as his horse and knew that he was sabotaged and

could not complete the fortification of Asgard. Thereupon, the Jötunn Builder was full of anguish and despair as his wall was impossible to complete in time with house his steed. Then, with wroth on his face, the Builder ripped off his robe and revealed he was a Giant in disguise. The Mason was unhappy, but the Æsir God led by the Alfahter, Odin agreed to pay him what he deserved. The Destroyer of Giants, Thor was within Asgard and pounded the God with his mighty hammer while his head was crushed into bloody breadcrumbs. Through the after-hours, the gods themselves completed the wall bit by bit. Loki was proud of what he did, and he departed into nightfall when he returned with Sleipnir, Odin's eight-legged horse.

1.5 THOR LOSES HIS HAMMER

I none of the best known poems Thyrmskvitha, it goes into detail of most eccentric Norse Mythology tale of how Thor lost his Hammer. One day, the halls of bilskirnir in Asgard, Thor laid in bed with his wife sif. As he roused out of bed he got his sacred belt known as Megingjörð, which means strength and power. Then he got his iron gloves, known as Járngreipr. But then he ventured over to get his happy he found a stark revelation that shook him to his core:

His enchanted Hammer known as MJölnir, was not in his room.

Not under the bed, not on his book shelf, not in his closet. His hammer had vanished like a lightning strike on a mountainside.

Thor was full of rage and he worried about the who what is the culprit who could yield this power to the doom of Asgard.

A Devastating divine Hammer he holds nearly as dear as his wife Sif. There, as the Asgard Kingdom trembled with Thor's fury, he found a random note on some parchment where he can find his Hammer. It was signed by **THRYM** (Tha-Rim) (Þrymr). He is a giant and was king of the Jötunn, a troll from the same breed as the aforementioned Manson Builder. Thor instantly thought of Loki, his typical deed of deception or thievery as any thinking God would do in this harrowing predicament. From the Payment, The Thunder God agreed to go to the land of giants, Jötunheim. Within the nightfall with the moon spilling down, he arrived at Thrym's palace. There within he saw Thrym in his decadent troll palace of lumbering trolls.

He said, *"Pease come closer as my eyes are not as good as they were in the past. You're now slimmer the last time we met."* Loki was there and saw the difference between the giant and Thor was massive.

Loki went to Asgard and negotiated Thrym's random and presented it to the tribe of Gods, the Æsir Gods. Then Thrym, the giant would give back in Hammer if Freya, the blonde beauty woman, would be his wife. The Gods were none too pleased with the proposal. Thor could not defend Asgard without the Hammer.

Then at very unusual request of trickery, Loki asked Thor unflinching and strange question. That would be this, for Thor to wear wedding dress of feathers. Thor was none-too-pleased to be asked that. Loki knew Thrym had poor sight and took advantage of that and wanted Thor to dress as a in a falcon feathered bridal dress of Freyja. He would be in disguise himself as a woman to trick Thrym that he was in fact the angelic god known as Freyja.

Thor, was in full Transvestism attire, to his own chagrin. The Thunder God awkwardly masqueraded down the halls dressed as a bride of feathers.

"Ugh, I can't wait until this day is over."

Then went to Thrym's palace by Chariot pulled by the goats Tanngrisnir and Tanngnjóstr. He arrived there and Thrym's companions were impressed. Thor was eager to get it over for the wedding feast and retrieved his Hammer once he detected it in the firelit shadows. The sprawling tables were lined with food, and the servants to deliver were many. Loki dressed as a servant of the Goddess Freyja. Thrym prepared a banquet for Thor, Dressed in Disguise as Freyja. Without problem, Thor voraciously ate all the food on the candle-lit table. Then, in a bit of a jest, Loki suggested they should consummate the union. Thrym agreed and then told his lackeys to bring   t h e Hammer. With his heart quaking and eyes peeled wide, Thor grabbed his Hammer from the thieves, consumed with rapacity. One by one, the Norse Thunder God smite all of the servants of the giants with his Hammer and broke Thrym's head open like a walnut. The blood oozed below the banquet tables.

When Thor wanted to get the female outfit off, Loki suggested,

"You look rather ravishing, Thor. The dress suits a Thunder God. Just don't have too much ale wearing that." He would mock Thor in the Valhalla Banquets when he dressed

like a bride. Within the poem Thyrmskvitha it would unfold like this:

"THINE SHOULD IT BE | THOUGH OF SILVER BRIGHT,
AND I WOULD GIVE IT | THOUGH 'TWERE OF GOLD."
THEN LOKI FLEW, | AND THE FEATHER-DRESS WHIRRED,
TILL HE LEFT BEHIND HIM | THE HOME OF THE GODS,
AND REACHED AT LAST | THE REALM OF THE GIANTS.

THEN HEIMDALL SPAKE, | WHITEST OF THE GODS,
LIKE THE WANES HE KNEW | THE FUTURE WELL:
"BIND WE ON THOR | THE BRIDAL VEIL,
LET HIM BEAR THE MIGHTY | BRISINGS' NECKLACE;

KEYS AROUND HIM | LET THERE RATTLE,
AND DOWN TO HIS KNEES | HANG WOMAN'S DRESS;
WITH GEMS FULL BROAD | UPON HIS BREAST,
AND A PRETTY CAP | TO CROWN HIS HEAD.

THE HEART IN THE BREAST | OF HLORRITHI LAUGHED
WHEN THE HARD-SOULED ONE | HIS HAMMER BEHELD;
FIRST THRYM, THE KING | OF THE GIANTS, HE KILLED,
THEN ALL THE FOLK | OF THE GIANTS HE FELLED.

1.6 LOKI'S CHILDREN

Throughout Norse Canon, many of the Gods had many female acquaintances and unions. Odin, the All-Father, had three. Loki himself was trying to be a good husband was married to **Sigyn.** (See-Gin) and had two children named **Nari** (Nar-ee) and Váli. (Vol-ee). She is a woman who would be steadfast and loyal to him even to the bitter end. They slept near Odin's eight-legged horse named Sleipnir and were part of "his offspring." Loki had female acquaintance cloaked in secret named **Angrboða**. (ANGA-BUDDA) and she lived in Jötunheim and so has the ominous moniker known as 'The Monster Of All Monsters." Angrboða and Loki would meet, and the method of precisely how they met, and copulated is not foretold. But what is known was the Roguish God and the Giantess would have a dreadful offspring unbeknownst to the rest of the Asgardians... until too late. They would be secret hellspawn offspring to the doom of the nine realms and bring about them the doorway to Doomsday.

There is a premonition from Elders that the Asgardians would go to battle with the forces of darkness, and Loki's offspring would be involved.

The vision involved a jaw on a massive wolf and then visions of omnipresent darkness about the worlds. Odin was worried about these tiding. Thus, he had a meeting with Loki to try to remedy these things that were foretold and to save kingdoms from bloodbaths and quaking in fear. They were trying to find more info about the son of Loki and catch him and his giant love affair offspring. Odin and the Gods left for Jötunheim to see the dwelling of the giant **Angrboða,** Loki's lover where would he would commit adultery within unknown darkness. The author would like to in Bela salon it'll bit who this giant was that Loki mothered, but there is little records about her beyond she was a giant.

Before the terrible prophecy could before, then Æsir God's kidnapped the children. Loki had animal offspring. One was a wolf cub named **Fenrir** (Fen-Re-Er), or Fenrisúlfr, which was a regular-sized cub. However, this animal was anthropomorphized. He communicated to the dogs in a common tongue after telling him what he would want as he grew.

The second was an ordinary snake, a serpent. It was

named **Jörmungandr,** the middle child of the two. The first part means *Jörmun-* for the word *gandr*. The Gandr refers to elongated supernatural beings. Loki's bastard child would grow brobdingnagian in size. Even encamping the entire sea. Thor and this snake would eventually become archfoes.

Loki had a fell daughter that was two face, one fair and one ghastly. The tormented offspring of Loki was named **Hel**. (Hell) with one side of the face like a rotting corpse as was the Goddess of Death. When the Gods went home Odin noticed the Serpent's size doubled to that of a Python. Odin decided to throw it into the great sea around Midgard. The tale grew into a monstrosity of size, and so much it encircled the whole world. The God's kidnapped them all to end the war as foretold by the evil that would befall the realm.

The snake Jörmungandr looked at Asgard with anger at Hel. It was frightened of her. Odin, the Alfather, noticed Hel liked the company of the dead more than the living. So he called her the Ruler of the World Dead known, also known as The Realm of Fire as **Musphelheim (or Helheim)**. She ruled over those who had an unworthy death and failed to reach Valhalla. The wolf cub named Fenrir was raised among the Gods of Asgard.

The son of a giant, a jötunn was God named **Týr** (Tear). Little beyond the superficial is known about this deity. But is written in archaic Scandinavian texts the immortal son of the jötunn bonded with the Fenrir. God of Perhaps, because he was the God of War and saw kinship with something so nefarious in disposition. But the Wolf pup kept growing to a monstrous nature of a nightmarish thing. Each hour, each day, and each month, Fenrir grew more and more and more in immensity. Thereafter, the wolf Fenrir was bigger than any animal that walked the earth. A giant among wolves. He said of became

more ill-favored and was becoming more wicked like Loki, his
father before him.

The tidings of this wolf's size spread like a wild fire and
there was trepidation growing within the Gods. In the halls of
Asgard, the god's would council of ways to wart of their own
doom. The Gods plotted ways to end the threat of the Wolf.
The God's would sit around a sprawling to table and discuss a
proper course of action. They reckon they must do something
as Thor stared at his table resting on the table with furrowed
brow. Loki would pace and and forth and he pled for the life of
his would.

"It is just a meek in benign wolf cub, it means nobody
any arm," Loki would plead.

Odin crossed his arm. "The prophecy says otherwise.
You bastard wolf child is a fell thing and will lead us... to
doom."

They bound the voracious monstrous Wolf with a
magical chain made of the beard of a woman, the breath of fish,
the sound of a cat's footsteps, and other occult elements.

Then the thoughtful Fenrir ended up breaking off the
chains. Odin taught the Gods to find a binding method in
the Land of the Dwarfs, Svartalfheim in the underground' of

Niðavellir. There, the dwarfs made something to contain the Demigod's offspring Fenrir. The increments were Mountain Roots, Bear Tendons, a woman's beard, a fish's breath and the bird's saliva, and The Sound of a Cat's Footsteps. They got that stuff, then gave the Gods a thin rope that looked made of silk and powerful.

They created "Gleipnir" the chain that put the island of Lyngvi until the war of the Gods known as Ragnarök. There was a prophecy that Loki's son Fenrir will bring about darkness. The Wolf kept growing and the dog's presented a challenge to Fenrir. But still a cub and liked playtime. They challenged him to get rid and were barely able to put him in chains as a challenge.

The Gods coiled Fenrir in it, and when he saw it he got angry as he became ensnared. Fenrir thought it was a trap and did not trust Odin, because he was Loki's son and knew a lie. The Wolf Fenrir said he would do it if one of the God dared to put their hands in hands in Wolf's mouth while tied up. If there was deception, he would devour God's hand right away. The Gods looked at one another and the Wolf got more suspicion with eyes of bloodlust.

Then Týr, the warrior god, agreed to the proposal. Then Týr. the one person who had a friendship with Fenrir, decided.

The Wolf snuggled and could not break out of the rope. Then looked at the Gods faces and saw Týr was the one who was not happy. He knew he was betrayed. A chain was placed on him and he bit off the hand of the God Týr. Then was tied to a stone like a fell monster. The Wolf was fierce and insulted the Gods. Many poems in Iceland and Norway about this climatic battle for the ages exist.

1.7 THOR'S ADVENTURE IN JÖTUNHEIMR

Loki and Thor crossed the world in Thor's Chariot. Through the endless wilderness, it was pulled by mighty goats named Tanngrisnir and Tanngnjóstr. They left together for the Kingdom of Giants, Jötunheim for new adventure and traveled eastward from Asgard's citadel.

They stopped at a small house for the night together and saw peasants and poor. They welcomed the Gods but had nothing to offer them. Thor slaughtered his goats for a meal and prepared it for the people. He asked for them to eat everything but leave the bones. Thor can bring the animal back to life if all the bones are intact. Loki decided to do plot of his antics on the deer meat. In the depth of the night, he approached the children of a children farmer. First, the son named **Thjalfi** (Thal-a-

fee), resoundingly fleet of foot young boy. He also had a sister named **Röskva** nearby.

He sought to corrupt the boy's goodness. Loki didn't like Thor got to keep all the marrow from the bones, a delicacy. Then he convinced the boy to try when everybody one asleep. In the act of betrayal, he broke one of the bones to taste the marrow. The bones were tossed over the skin of the dead frothing in blood. Thor brought the Goats back to life, his ritual. But he noticed one of the animals was limping, his leg was broken like a wishbone. Thor was outraged and reached out for his hammer. He was curious and felt betrayed that a bone was snapped. Loki had a hidden smirk and Thjalfi confessed of the crime. The Heathen Thunder God wanted to destroy the house and looked at Thjalfi with rage.

Thjalfi said it was him,

"Sir, please. I beg you. Spare my family and my sister I'll be your servant to pay debt." Thor relented and was benevolent and spared the boy's life. Though, he would have to treat his goats. Thor, Thjalfi and his sister Röskva, and Loki left to explore the hinterlands of the giants of Jötunheim. Through the intense cold, they entered a mammoth cave and ducked inside as the merciless snow was unrelenting. Within the cave they heard

something tremble the heard and Thor stepped outside. A huge giant slept beside the cave, and snoring shook everything around them. The giant wore only one glove named **Skrymir.** (Sker-Mirror). They learn that the other glove they were in was in fact... The Cave.

When the mammoth lumbering giant pulled his glove Thor, Thjalfi and Loki fell out of Skrymir's glove on the stone floor. He then told the threesome who he was, Skrymir.

Then said, *"I can serve as your guide and also carry your luggage."* They accepted the offer, having not known the region very well and carried their stuff. The giant got tired and decided to take a nap. Then night came and they all got hungry. They tried to open the sleeping giant's bag. Thor beat the giant in the head with his hammer to wake him. He felt it was only a leaf. Skrymir went back to sleep. Dawn was ebbing over the hillside and were starving for their own breast fast in the giant's bag. The giant kept sleeping and Thor him in the head with all his might with his hammer. He woke up like he was pestered by a bug.

The giant told their sedition with where at the castle of **Útgarðar**, in Old Norse Útgarðr. It is the stronghold of trolls, known in Norse Paganism as jötnars. **Útgarða-Loki,**

was the ruler of the castle Útgarðr in Jötunheim His name was a troll, a Jötnar. **Útgarða-Loki**, the name means "Loki of the Outyards." It's this ruler that called the giant Skrymir soft and weak. Thor went to the giant's palace but sensed perpetual unease about being in a haven of trolls. The Thunder God was worried because the giants were bigger than Skrymir, as he was bulled around. Through the journey through the day breaking, they arrive at the giant's castle in mid-afternoon to explore the castle of Útgarðar.

All of the Asair Gods entered the castle to see the giants living there. The Lord of the Palace, Útgarða-Loki, challenged them to beat them at anything. Loki was going to face **Logie**, the giant's servant. So in those halls he challenges Loki in a baritone voice,

"Who can eat the banquet the fastest?"

Loki started eating all the food fast at the same time. The giant ate the bones, platters cutlery and was declared the winner. As his sister Röskva, stood back in the shadows, Thjalfi said he would race against anybody within the castle. Útgarða-Loki found a challenger quickly. The sprinter boy went against a giant boy in an epic foot race. He was no match for the giant. Thor had three challenges. Drink everything in a huge horn at

one go. Thor was confident he could do it; drinking is one of his skills. He reached his limit but only drank a small part of it. The next one was Thor lifting his pet cat. The cat was very heavy, and Thor struggled but left it over his head but its paws still touched the ground. The Final Challenge was to fight the giant's foster mother and old woman. A giantess.

Thor needed a win, and felt the old lady giant and he was still defected in a close struggle. The Gods left and the giants followed them to the threshold of Asgardian's borders. Then, the giant they met, **Skrymir**, confessed the border: he fooled them all. He was in fact, the King of the Giants. Furthermore, he used magic and went order hit him with a mountain that turned into a valley.

Then he told Loki he was competing against a magical fire that consumed everything in its path.

Thjalfi, was competing against the concept of "thought" and nothing was faster than that. Thor wondered what enchantment was used against him and he pressed him for answers.

The horn that he used was connected to the ocean. So he had no chance but did bring the sea level down two meters. Thor was not lifting a cat, but rather Jörmungand, the world's serpent thats transfigured into a cat—-Thor was humiliated. The fact he could lift it off the ground was quite the feat. Most surprisingly, Thor almost defeated the older woman, who was OLDNESS itself. And time, Thor was fed up with the shenanigans. He wanted to kill the giant, but he used his magic to vanish with his castle. Thor returned to Asgard and knew everything he did was impossible to defeat but one: Jörmungand, the world's biggest snake. Thor wanted to cross paths with the thing known as the World's Snake again.

1.8 THE FATE OF BALDR AND LOKI

T his chapter chronicles one of the great stories that led to the series of events that would lead to the climatic event Ragnarök. Various stanza within Vegtamskviða is an Eddic poem, that would go into cryptic detail about what transpired. But the most famous of which was *Baldrs draumar (dreams)*. It was written in the mid-10th century and appeared in the AM 748 I 4to, a vellum manuscript, which means a manuscript made out of animal skin. The following poem recounts Baldr's death goes like so.

Odin's wife's name is **Frigg,** goddess of clairvoyance, also known as a völva, which is a Norse name for a Seeress. Odin and Frigg had Four sons and Gods, Thor, Baldr, Víðarr, and Váli. Her son Baldr was joyful and communicated happiness of life. He was the beloved of all gods and also impervious to any harm,

for he was the immortal god of the Æsir tribe. However, when night came his sleep was consumed by terrible nightmares of his own fate.

Baldr's beloved wife Naina (Na-NA) and No God knew the reason for Baldr's nightmares. An Oracle told Odin told there is help from the Kingdom of Hell known as Helheim, a place here Hel, a double-faced disformed woman and daughter of Loki who presides of it. Odin, took the runes, and disguised himself as a wanderer with a wide brim hat. Through many leagues he traveled and went to the Kingdom of the Dead, known as Helheim. A Völva told Odin, a seer, they are preparing themselves to receive Baldr.

The sadness swept over Asgard, the Heathen Gods were crestfallen and needing reconciliation—-except for Loki. Baldr's noble spirit would be in the pits of the underworld of Helheilm. Though in Norse Mythology Hell is not like the Christian hell. Helleim is not a place of evildoers. Within the Scandinavian-originated originated Hell, it is a place in the afterlife for souls who died of old age and the less remarkable lives of everyday common folk.

With news of these ominous prophetic tidings, Odin returned to Asgard with the news of the fate of Baldr. The Goddess Frigg,

a Völva, a seer was overcome with sorrow. In her grief, she had everybody swear they would never hurt her beloved son. Even weapons and diseases and plants committed not to hurt him. But at the same time, Loki was deeply jealous, overflowing of love and attention for Baldr but reluctantly agreed.

The Gods were amused and threw spears at him and did nothing. The hammer of Thor did nothing. They were all happy to know he was protected. Like the sun rises in the east, and sets in the west, events in Norse Mythology are predestined and cannot be altered.

Loki was none too pleased and was determined to find a vulnerability. He disguised himself as the goddess Frigg and told her friend about the oath. He learned everything went into the oath except for the Mistletoe, which was harmless. Loki's evil agenda work in full force. He found some Mistletoe as they were testing Baldr for weakness with blades.

Loki created a Dart made of Mistletoe in an absurdly tragic event and went to Baldr. He said his blinds would not harm him. So Loki went invisible in the dark. Baldr joined the prank. Loki threw the dart at Baldr with full force. Silence grew about the kingdom: mummers and silence. Fort the dart stuck Baldr and he bled out and fell like a stuck pig.

All about everywhere, the Gods and Goddess lamented his death. They would be candlelight vigil for the vanquished as the Heaven Gods were in morning. The Punishment Of Loki The Gods were not happy with Loki's evil schemes in the most beloved and revered of all Vanir Gods. So they sent the messenger of Gods named **Hermóðr**, (HERM-A-THOR) to the Kingdom of Hell. They wanted him to go there to bring him back from the dead. Hel, the woman with two faces from the underworld, agreed to return Baldr as they lamented God's death. Everybody in Asgard was summoned to get a confirmation to get God back.

However, there was a giantess in the mountains who did not want his return or was engulfed in sorrow. They learned Baldr could not return because of that one holdout. They learned the heartless giantess was in fact... Loki. The Heathen Gods were at a wit's end. They were sick of Loki's wrongdoings and conniving tricks as he fled for the outskirts of sight. They wanted him banished from the pantheon of Gods. The deities combed the earth looking for him. At last, when hope was lost. Odin could see the whole world from his throne and saw Loki's hiding spot in the mountains in a Salmon filled well. Knowing his capture was drawing here, Loki used his guile and thought quickly and fled. He remained elusive and used skills like a necromancer. He

used his talents of Hamrammr and shapeshifted into a Salmon and went with the fish form and swam into the river known as Franang's Falls. As he fled capture and fended for his life, Loki found a mass of strings could catch a fish in the first fishing net ever. When Loki saw the Gods were coming, he threw the fishnet into a fire and jumped into it. They saw him jump into the river.

As they headed into the cavern at the bottom of the waterfall, the **Kvasir**, the wisest of all the Æsir saw the fishnet in the mains of the fire.

The Gods made various nets to capture Loki in the water and decided they needed to construct a new net to capture the God. One by one, he miraculously dodged these nets with divine skill. Thor thought if a bear could get a salmon during a jump, Loki would too, in that enchanted form. Thus, Loki was captured by Thor in fish form as he jumped in the air in Franang's Falls and was caught as they dragged it in the water.

With eyes full of wraith a heart of rage, the Norse deity of Wickedness went back to human form in terror of Thor. Upon capturing the trickers God Loki, the Æsir Gods wanted to publish Loki. So they found the God of vengeance, **Vali**. He one of the sons of Odin and the giantess **Rindr**. The Æsir Gods

transformed him into a fierce wolf, and he ate Loki's son, Narvi. Then, they used Narvi's entrails and tied Loki down in a cave grotesque calculating medieval torture manner.

They all wanted to kill him but Odin digressed, for he had a Blood Pact with him. They were like Asgardian brothers. He would not allow the death of Loki, the son of the giant Fárbauti. The goddess of skiing, Skadi (Old Norse: Skaði) hung, and had stalactite over his head. From there, she hug a humongous snake from a spike and the Venom fell on him and burned his face to agony for the ages of infinity. The mischievous God was angry. His fell heart was set on the seeds of revenge.

With the prophecy of the twilight of gods known as Ragnarök drawing near, Loki's wife, **Sigyn**, (SIG-EM) stayed by his side while he got even more punishment. In the darkness, as we were chained, she tried to calm him by using a bowl to catch the Venom of the snake over him that was disfiguring his face like acid. In that dank cavernous dwelling, the bowl got full of Venom and she washed it away with her undying love for her husband. The Venom fell on him again, and he belted a scream that echoed through the subterranean darkness. The most infamous heathen God declared revenge for all the suffering that happened to him. This was the first chain of events that would

bring about the Twilight of the Gods, known in the cataclysmic event known as Ragnarök. As written in the forward, there was no basic book of scripture to encompass all these tales. Many of the following events are contradictory and cryptic. Rudolf Simek, an Austrian philologist and religious studies living today, believes the 13th century historical and politician Snorri Sturluson invented the following's lake's name. Within the lake of Ámsvartnir is the island of lyngvi. On that island, the terrible wolf and Loki's Fenrir remained chained in the enchanted chain known as Gleipnir. It had its mouth propped open and the droll came down that created a river known as Ván (In Old Norse that translates to "hope")

1.9 ÞJAZI (THJAZI)

According to Skáldskaparmál, one day the gods Odin, Loki and Henir set off across mountains and wilderness until they needed food. In a valley, they saw a herd of cows and put one of them in an earthen oven, but after a while they found that it was not cooked. As they tried to determine the cause, they heard a voice in the oak tree overhead, saying that it was his own fault that the stove hadn't boiled. They looked up and there was Þjazi in the form of a great eagle and he told them that if they let him eat the cow, he would put the stove on the boil. They agreed, so he came down from the tree and started gobbling. Þjazi ate too much, Loki got angry and grabbed his long cane to hit him, but the weapon was stuck firmly to Þjazi, and he ran away, hugging Loki up. As they flew throughout the land Loki shouted and begged to be permit down as his legs banged towards timber and stones, however Þjazi could most effective accomplish that at the situation that Loki should trap Iðunn out of Asgard together along with her apples of youth,

which he solemnly promised to do. Later, at the appointed time, Loki lures Iduon from Asgard to a forest, and tells her that he has found some apples that she may consider valuable, and that she should bring her own apples for comparison. Þjazi then appears in the form of an eagle, catches Iðunn and flies with her to his kingdom of Þrymheimr in Jötunheimr. The gods who were deprived of the Apple of Iðunn began to grow old and gray. After learning that Iðunn was last seen leaving Asgard with Loki, they threatened him with torture and death until he agreed to rescue them. Loki borrows a magic cloak from Freyja that turns him into a falcon, and flies to Jotunheim until he reaches the Hall of Þjazi. When Þjazi sailed out to sea, Loki found Iðunn alone, he transformed her into a nut, carried her back, and flew as fast as he could.

When Þjazi returned home to find her missing, he changed into eagle form and flew towards Loki. Seeing Loki flying towards them with Þjazi, the gods ignited Þjazi's feathers, causing him to fall to the ground, attacked and killed. Þjazi's daughter Skadi then dons her war gear and travels to Asgard for revenge, but the gods offer her atonement and compensation until she is appeased. She was also married to Njord, and as further compensation, Odin removed Þjazi's eyes and placed them in

the night sky as stars.

Also according to Skáldskaparmál, the father of Þjazi and his brothers Gangr and Idi was named Olvaldi. Olvaldi was so rich in gold that after his death his three sons divided their inheritance among them, each taking a bite in turn. Because of this, the phrases "the speech of Þjazi, Gangr, or Idi" and "Idi's luminous talk" are synonymous with gold, and in the same book, Þjazi is twice given the pronoun of "wolf girl", referring to It was he who was kidnapped by Iðunn. The other was the "caretaker of the Snowshoe God" or father of the Snow Goddess.

1.10 THE MARRIAGE OF NJORD AND SKADI

T he story begins with the kidnapping of Eaton and ends. As the gods celebrated their slaying of the giant Þjazi and the return of the youth-giving goddess Iden to their halls, an unexpected visitor burst into their merriment. This is Skadi, the giantess, who comes with armor and weapons to avenge the death of her father Þjazi. The gods were patient with her and persuaded her to accept compensation rather than seek revenge. This compensation is divided into three parts. First, Odin cast Þjazi's eyes solemnly into the night sky, turning them into two stars.

Skadi couldn't help but chuckle when she saw this. First, the gods tried to make Skadi laugh by performing various humorous tasks. None of them succeeded. Loki tied one end of a rope to a goat and the other end around his testicles. He tugged on the rope, pulling the goat along. Third, Skadi was to be given a god

of her choosing in marriage, but she was to select him by the sight of his feet and legs alone. She saw the fairest pair of feet she could see, thinking they were those of Baldur. However, as it turned out, they were those of the sea-god Njord. After their magnificent wedding, it was time for the newlyweds to decide where to live. Njord's home was Noatun (the "place of ships"), a bright, warm place on the beach. Skadi's home was Thrymheim (the "thunder-home"), a dark, foreboding place in the highest mountain peaks where the snow never melts. The couple first spent nine nights in Thrymheim. When this time had passed and they made their way down from the mountains, Njord declared that, although brief, his time in Thrymheim had been unpleasant. He had been disturbed by the sounds of the wolves, which he overwhelmingly preferred the songs of the swans to which he was accustomed.

1.11 THE BEGINNING OF RAGNARÖK AND THE DOOM OF THE GODS

Theeschatonfor the ages is known in the Heathen Cannon as Ragnarök. This essentially means the Apocalypse of the Gods in the world at large. In the Scandinavian religion, this is the most grandiose mythological story of the whole Region. Filled with monstrous things and epic battles and blood-soaked fields. A climatic event would be the staple of the whole mythic tale of good and evil. This Earth shattering event of norse mythology is prophecy of what is to come. So in theory, present time is this very chapter and all befalls after it a prophecy of an impending apocalypse. It would be called other times such a *"aldar rök"* which translate to "fate of mankind."

All the Vellum parchment, Eddic poems and word of

mouth whispers among Vikings, it was spoken that God's are stand still before the day of reckoning. One of the most referred pieces of art about this topic is Richard Wagner, the 18th century classical composer. His opera named Götterdämmerung is the German translation of the word 'Ragnarök' and the ominous sounding "twilight of the gods."

Within the halls of Asgard, the All Father himself, Odin whispered of the tidings. The immortal Gods had mortal fear. They had trepidation of the prophecy and the ramifications of it. That when the mythological wolves **Sköll and Hati** devour the son of the moon and the world will, he be covered in a veil of darkness. Also, the God's knew that Loki's wolf son Fenrir and serpent son Jörmungandr would lead to their own doom.

It was now within the prelude to the war of all wars. The Gods were within equals states of puzzlement and dissolution to hinder this defeat. In the Halls of Asgard, knew they would force the faces of evil during Ragnarök and were not everlasting. Midgard was the land of the first descents of **ASK** and **EMBLA**, the first humans shielded them from the forces of chaos by Thor and his hammer. Dark tiding were coming but they caught to protect humanity. The humans never forgot to pay their proper sacrifices to the Gods and had keen awareness of

the toll of the endless stretches of winter of three long winters called **Fimbulvinter.** An unexpected frost hurt the crops way before they should have. Crops were ruined as they prepared for a brutal winter that showed no mercy. It was foretold there would be three winters without a summer in-between. T h e y feared the sun may never come again. They were forced to eat egg-producing chicken and their pets. If they hunted, they are prey to the pack of Fenrir, Loki's huge wolf son. With hope dwindling, brother fought brother and children fought parents and the battlefield of immortal and mortal blood and blood slathered axes and swords. The ultimate battle between the Gods and chaos were brewing and the Twilight of the Gods had come to fruition. However parts of the prophecy would be the whole world would be swallowed up by oceans and most all life would be lost.

Then three roosters would crow, and they would know the giants would come. The Fjalar, Gullinkambi, and another unnamed one lived in Hel. Each of them prophesies the dead will rise from Helheilm and Ragnarök shall begin and Loki has escaped his torment. They know that the battle will begin at a field of Vígríðr or Óskópnir and the Apocalypse of the deities is on the verge of unfolding. **Einherjar**, 800 of the most revered

Dead Spirit Warriors will come from Valhalla to just the Æsir Gods in this battle for all nine realms.

After three never-ending winters, chaos and blood were everywhere. The prophecy was true about the beginning of the end with Ragnarök. Two wolves who said they were the offspring of Fenrir went across the sky near the sun and moon. Haidee (hay-dee), one of the wolves, chased the moon. The second wolf, Skull, chased the sun. The celestial deities who repented time escaped them. The wolves swallowed them. The tree of the world, Yggdrasil, then trembled.

A mighty crack in the mountain came. Fenrir, and the way he was bound in the enchanted rope, was shattered, and the fell was free. Jörmungandr, shook in a quake in the waters that caused gargantuan waves. It released position into the waters. Whales and fish and even plankton all died.

Loki was in prison in the drank cavernous dwelling with the leering snake on stalagmites over him, the chains were broken in the chaos of the Apocalypse. He said in a chilly breathe,

"Now the freedom to wreak havoc and... the freedom for revenge."

He sought revenge and went to Helheim, the kingdom of hell for

those with an unworthy death for recruitment in the war of the ages. The Queen of the Dead, Hel, gave her father an army of the undead of Nordic Zombies known as the **Níðhöggr**, the dragon that eats the roots of the tree of world, Yggdrasil, dug a tunnel for the army of undead. Then many terrible things came from a haven of inferno **Muspelheim.** The army of Musphelheim marched through flames.

In some of the more nightmarish imagery in all of North Mythology is the ship known as the Naglfar, the terrible ship fashioned after the fingernails of the dead docked and moored on a shoreline. At the helm, it was commandeered by the **Hrym**, a jötnar with all the giants on board. With a second ship, supplied by Hel, it was captained by the now escaped Loki. With the lower decks was the terrible fire giant.

This chief jötunn ushered from the ash and fire world and was led by a giant named **Surtr** (Search-er) The Black. He is known as the "he swarthy one." He is the half-brother of Ymir, the frost giant in who lived in the realm embedded in ice known as Niflheim. It is said this mammoth fire giant was one thousand feet tall and power of transfiguration. His father fingers could could be changed into that of a serpent. Ymir, was of course, ripped apart to create the world by Odin as his

brother. He also was Audhumbla, the opening chapter's comic creation cow's half-brother. This fire demon incarnate dwells in the place of an inferno in the nether regions of the world, the domain of all the fallen fire giants. The flaming region of Muspel certainly has some distinct similarities to it, but it was more of a place for common folk and the lame rather than the wicked.

Within this furnace underworld, the giant Surtr was the arbitrator of all the evil that grew there. Since the dawn of time, he had been working in the fiery fords and constructing of the ultimate weapon of a sword of flame known as the **Sól Valtiva**. For thousands of years, he has had a singular goal to set the universe on fire with his fell sword of the inferno on the battlefield of Ragnarök.

The calamitous evil fire giant scorched everything in his path with a blade of the inferno. The giants of Jötunheim, the ice giants, boarded the ships made of people's nails. This ship was called Naglfar. So the battle began in the battleground between Gods and forces of unchained chaos.

In Midgard was the land of the first descents of ASK and EMBLA, the Æsir Gods attended to the first humans. As the battle was almost at hand, they shielded themselves from the forces of

chaos with Thor and his hammer as they hid away in the colossal world tree, Yggdrasil. The humans never forgot to pay their proper sacrifices to the Gods and the men were keenly aware of the stitches of winter. Which was this, three long winters called **Fimbulvinter**. They knew they would force the faces of evil during Ragnarök and were not everlasting. An unexpected frost hurt the crops way before they should have. Crops were ruined by they prepared for a brutal winter.

Three winters came without a summer in-between. They feared the sun might never come again and the world may forever be embedded in frost. They were forced to eat egg-producing chicken and their pets. If they hunted they are prey to the pack of Fenrir, Loki's huge wolf son. With hope dwindling like a fading candlelight, the brother fought brother, and children fought parents as mankind was in pandemonium. Swords were doused in blood, axes dripped blood, and the mortal's blood waxed in the moon's waxing light.

The ultimate battle between the Gods and chaos was brewing, and the Twilight of the Gods had come to fruition.

Odin and the Æsir god's all feared the prophecy that when the Mythological wolves Skoll and Hati devour the son of the moon and the world will he be cloaked in blinding darkness.

Then three roosters would crow and they would know the giants will come, and the dead will rise from Helheilm. Ragnarök has begun and Loki has escaped his torment.

The God named **Heindel** (Hine-Del), the guardian of the Gods, saw Ragnarök had begun. He blew the Gjallarhorn and heard throughout the universe. This was the end of **Azurian** (Eye-Sy-ri-an) Gods, the oldest and greatest of all the Gods and the end of the Gods was here as the Apocalypse, and the final destiny of the Gods had come to fruition in nightmarish reality.

1.12 RAGNARÖK AND THE DOOM OF THE GODS

After three never-ending winters, chaos and blood were everywhere as the world's fate was challenged. The prophecy was true about the beginning of Ragnarök and end of the World. One of the quandaries, when one examines this mythic tale, is Odin's treatment of Loki's wolf, Fenrir, the enormous snake Jörmungand and two-faced daughter Hel in such an uncouth manner. Did he (or will) Odin bring about Ragnarök? Was that overused puppy mistreated by being chained? Was Hel's banishment to Helheim justified? Should that monstrous serpent be tossed into the sea? If one thinks about it, intellectualize these stories in an antagonist and protagonist matter; from this author's perspective, two of three were unjustified.

First that springs to me is the wolf Fernier. He was

anthropomorphized, he had human consciousness and could talk. Thus, one could conclude certainly be construed as intelligent. He sensed being betrayed when he was chained up on the island of Lyngvi after he bit off the hand of God Týr. However, if you put your hand into an angry wolf's mouth, what bloody aftermath is expected. Encapsulation, the wolf Fenrir, seed to be the most misunderstood antagonist in all of Norse Legends. From this author's perspective, maybe chaining up that wolf wasn't the best plan for all nine realms to thwart an apocalypse.

In terms Loki's doubled faced half-goddess-, half-jötunn daughter Hel, who was banished to the after realm, also was a little harsh. Perhaps that is just a modern thought process on the banishment of women. But that leviathan, Jörmungand was certainly not gonna be the act in a civil manner and that cursed thing needed to be defeated. But if there is one character in all of Norse mythos which is irredeemable, irresponsible, and the personification of evil, that would certainly be Loki. He is like if Judas in the Bible was a God who likes mischievous antics to all of those who he met. Most for paradoxically, he's easily forgiven almost each and every time. The One Father himself was certainly too lenient on such a mischievous double-crossing

dastardly deity. Of course, in Norse pathology, or processes are pre-destined and cannot be changed. These are ancient stories with ancient ways of thinking. So it's best not to intellectualize them too much and enjoy the legends embedded throughout the culture for thousands of years. They stand the test of time because they are myths that spark the imagination like a candlelight vigil in a cave.

Two wolves who said they were the offspring of Loki's wolf child Fenrir. They would traverse across the sky near the sun and moon. **Haidee** (hay-dee), one of the wolves, chased the moon. The second wolf, Skull chased the sun. The celestial deities who repented time escaped them. The wolves swallowed them.

The tree of the world, Yggdrasil, with roots deep and the humans Ask and Embla would be full of consternation for the chaos that will unfold. The Great Tree trembled as a battle for the ages drew near. A mighty crack in the mountain came. Fenrir, and the way he was bound, was shattered. Jörmungandr shook in waters and caused waves. It released position into the waters. Whales and fish and even plankton all died from the tumultuous event. Loki was in prisoned in that ominous cavern with the venomous snake leering on him, had his chains broke

and the manner his freedom is not wholly clear. He sought revenge and embarked on quest to Helheim, the kingdom of hell for those with an unworthy death. The Queen of the Dead, Hel, gave her father an army of the undead of Nordic Zombies Níðhöggr, the dragon that devoured the roots of the tree of the world, Yggdrasil, dug a tunnel for the army of undead. The army of Musphelheim was marching through flames. Einherjar, Eight hundred of the most revered Dead Spirit Warriors will come from Valhalla to just the Æsir Gods in this battle for all nine realms.

The battle began in the battleground between Gods and forces of chaos.

Heimdall's horn announced that Ragnarök had started to end the Azur Gods. The Azurian Gods prepared for thousands of years. The huge golden Gates of Valhalla were opened and thousands of warriors stepped out of the hall. They formed Odin's great army to assail his foes. They were the bravest army of all nine realms. They were taken by the **Valkyries**, a version of flying angelic to the hall of Valhalla, where they waited the battle of all battles. These humans fought with the Gods during this time shoulder to shoulder. The giants of Musphelheim tried to shatter the Asgardian gates and pinwheel of color bridge Bilröst

collapsed in the process of the havoc. With that bridge broke in the momentous chaois in the end of all things, the prophecy said part of the army fell into the icy waters.

The giants drowned in the waters. The Gods knew their destiny was to face the forces of darkness, not hide. Odin, grew upon his league of Gods and formed an army known as the Einherjar. He mounted his eight-legged horse and ordered the attack upon the giants of Musphelheim. When they clashed the tree of the world, Yggdrasil, trembled. Thor smashed thousands of giants. Hyrum led the ice giants during this battle against Odin's army.

Loki guided Hel's army of undead from the afterrealm.

In the battle of all battles in the field of **Vígríðr** (or **Vigrid)**, the Æsir and Giants fought for the world. The Venire God fought bravely with his golden bore with the Asgardians. Freyr, God who belongs to the Vanir tribe of deities and ruled one of nine realms known as Vanaheim. The god was associated with sunshine and had the **Sumarbrander**, Sword of Freyr, before he gave it away so thought-provoking in name but his sorely underwritten in Norse legends.

So within that battle field for the ages, set fourth against the firestorm of a giant Surtr. With savaged life or death blows,

he Freyr attacked the leader of the giants. In the end, Surtr was killed Freyr with his flaming sword. But in a whirlwind of death and live, when things swing back and forth like a pendulum, Freyr was the first to a parish on the battlefield. The exact nature of his demise remains unclear.

Then Týr, the warrior god, then fell facing the powerful wolfman named **GARN**, a wolf from nightmares. He defended the world of the dead. **Týr** (*tear*) stuck his sword into the hellish beast's heart before he died. Then the serpent of the world, Jörmungand appeared ready to kill. It released venomous gas that killed the warriors of Odin. Nevertheless, Thor was confident and waited for the final battle with Loki's bastard brood sea serpent that lurked in the World Sea's fathomless abyss.

The slithering Leviathan tried to swallow Thor, but he hit the massive snake with his hammer and it sank into the ground with a lethal strike to the head. But in that aftermath of that blow, it also hit Jörmungand. From that poison pockets spread all about the battlefield and a venomous cloud went around Thor. The Thunder God fell to his knees and dead from poison coursing through his veins.

With the ultimate champion, it was more difficult for

the Gods. Fenrir, the enormous wolf as tall as twenty men, devoured all those who attacked him and spit out their bones. The wolf wanted to kill Odin, his nemesis. Odin knew it was his destiny to fight the terrifying wolf. Odin rode his eight-legged horse, **Sleipnir** (SIPHON-NEAR) advanced to fight the fell wolf of nightmares.

The terrible mammoth wolf devoured the father of all, Odin.

The wolf mocked the Gods for killing Odin. Vidar, the son of Odin was filled with mourning and rage and attacks the colossal wolf. As the wolf tried to eat him whole like a tasty morsel. Vidar stuck his feet into the wolf's tongue. He tore the once thought-of indomitable wolf's jaw asunder. The bane of the gods was dead. Loki was satisfied with the carnage on the battlefield, though his son died. **Heindel,** (Hind-dallll) the guardian of the rainbow bridge of Bilröst. Advanced on the army of the undead towards Loki. Heindel and Loki did a deadly dance duel and both killed one another.

Surtr burned the world with his sword in anger. There we no fightings on the side of the living. Only ashes remained. Then Asgard's rampart crumbled and it was consumed by rivers of fire. Oceans rose and started to flood. The twilight had fallen on the corpse's of the Æsir Gods, their reign was over. Things

went back to normal but all was died. The World Tree, Yggdrasil welted away and died. Within the tree of Yggdrasil was a few mortal beings. So the humans were in there, and their world was repopulated. The Great cataclysm known as Ragnarök was at end. Without the work of Snorri Sturolson many of these myths would be lost in the darkness of history. For all writers, storytellers and people searching for guidance, may this man rest in peace for removing the vail of shadows on all of these legends.

ODIN - "The father of all" or "All-father God" in Norse Mythology. He was also known as Woden, Odinn, Wuodan, Woutan, Wodnesdeeg, the Day of Odin. (Modern Word "Wednesday", the weekday that was named after him). He stands at the top of the Aesir pantheon of all Gods. Beloved, well known throughout the world. Fierce and powerful. Odin's true gift was his thirst for knowledge of all affairs. So much so that he had two ravens named **Hugin and Munin**, they gave Odin tidings of the world.

He looked after the nine realms from the day of their creation until the end of the Norse Myths. He once impaled his heart

with the mighty Gungnir Spear (GUN-SHEAR) and hung from the World Tree for a staggering nine days and nine nights to gain knowledge of the mystical abilities of runes and all of the magic and wisdom within. He also ripped his eye out. He was a womanizer and enjoyed the company of many goddesses and giantess and Jötnars.

Another thing: he had a flying, eight-legged steel horse called **Sleipnir.** Finally, he had a spear named **Gungnir.**

FRIGG - (or **Frigga**) Odin's wife. She is the matriarch of the Aesir pantheon. She had the power of knowledge and foreknowledge and prophecy. She could see what could happen to everyone and everything. She even saw Ragnarok. After a prophecy came of his demise, she asked for anybody to swear an oath never to hurt her son. However, she missed mistletoe. Loki used that as a way to kill him in a game of darts. Events in Norse Mythology are predestined and cannot be changed, beloved by all people, and associated with fertility, marriage, motherhood, and domestic stability.

Jörð - (pronounced Your). Another name: **Fjörgyn**. The word means earth and land. The personification of the earth. Sexual

partner of Odin. Mother of Thor. She is known as a giantess. She was Odin's Side Chick.

Mímir - Mímir renowned for his knowledge and wisdom. In a terrible turn of events for him, he was decapitated during the Æsir–Vanir War. Afterward, Odin uses herbs to bring his head back to life. Then he carried his head and it recited secret knowledge and counsel to him. He is Odin's Uncle.

LOKI, (Or Loke) the God of mischief. Odin's brother. Son of the giant Fárbauti. He is Thor's Uncle. Odin's brother. He had two kids that were a massive wolf and a world size snake. Pure evil, sabotages everything through trickery. He has two children he made with a Giantess. He also is a **Jötunn**, (Yo-din) (or normal spelling **Jötun**). Basically, negative being. A contrasting person of the Gods. His deeds set forth Ragnarok.

Angrboða - Loki impregnated this giantess and spawned two hellish creatures that played into the events of Ragnarok. She is the mother of monsters. Also, he is only mentioned once in the Poetic Edda (Völuspá hin skamma). She also is known as "Wise Woman of the Ironwood."

JORMUNGANDR - (Your Man Gonder) The son of Loki. The world serpent. A snake that is big as the world. One was a common snake, a serpent. It was named Jörmungand. It plays into Ragnarok and the twilight of the Gods.

FENRIR - (or **Fenrisúlfr.**) The other son of Loki and giantess, **Angrboða.** Fenrir, the huge wolf, devoured all those who attacked him. During Ragnarok, he fought with Loki on the side of the Jötunn and other monsters. He was put into a magical chain by Tyr, and he was told o put his hand in his mouth to prove he wasn't being tricked. He bit Tyr's hand off. The wolf wanted to kill Odin, his nemesis. He also kills the goddess of the underworld known as Hel.

HEL - Goodness - Was the ruler of the Norse Underworld **HELHEIM.** Or, Hell's Kingdom. Her siblings were the world serpent **JORMUNGANDR** and the huge world **FENRIR—dysfunctional** family. The place she dwells in Helheim is quiet and gloomy. Nordic people went there after their death not because they were evil but because they died of old age. Essentially, this place was an uneventful afterlife. On the other end, Valhalla and Fólkvangr, were more equivalent to

the Christian Heaven and for those who did more adventurous things and got exciting afterlife.

BALDUR - The beloved son of Odin. Also, the half-brothers of Thor. Wise, beloved by all (except Loki) and handsome. More beautiful than "any flower." Balder's Achilles heel was mistletoe and that is how he died from his twin brother. However, he would return from the dead after the events of Ragnarok.

Hodr - (Pronounced Ho-Der) Other Odin offspring, blind. Loki tricked him into killing Balder by using the mistletoe when he was blind with a dart in his hand. He did not know it was a mistletoe in his hand.

THOR - God of thunder, and has a hammer called Mjölnir. The most famous Norse God. He protects Asgard from evil with his power of thunder but is usually thwarted by Loki. Belt of Megingjarder. Mother's name is Jörð. Wife's name is SIF. Some Germanic myths say **Fjorgyn** is his mother. He is Asgard's staunch defender. He would ride in a chariot drawn by two giant goats. His crowning achievement: killing the world serpent, Jörmungandr. But, he is killed moments later by the

venom. The day Thursday is titled after him.

SIF - The Wife of Thor and was associated with mother earth, just like Thor's mother, JOR. She was known for golden hair that Loki cut in a trick. Thor demented her hair back. So Loki had to find her hair.

VALI - A son of Odin and the **Giantess Rindr**. He was born to avenge the death of his brother, **BALDUR.** So he took his vengeance on Loki. Vali binds Loki in the entrails of Loki's Son, Narfi. Vali grew to adulthood within a day. Then he lived in Asgard with the rest of the Aesir Gods. He was also prophesied to be one of the survivors of Ragnarok along with his brother, Vidar.

VIDAR - The God of Vengeance. He is the son of Odin and Jötunn Grid. His name means "wide ruler." He is known as a silent God—actions made up for it. Vidar is the one who killed the wolf in Ragnarok named Fenrir, Loki's son, and avenged his father's death. Also, one of the very few Asgardian Gods to miraculously survive the calamity of Ragnarok. He lived on the field of Idavoll after the battle for the beginning of a new world.

Ymir - Not exactly a god; he is the center of Norse Myth creation of all things. When the fires of Ginnungagap melted, Ymir, the gargantuan frost giant and Audhumla, the cosmic cow at the creation of the nine realms. He is of extreme importance. He is a cosmic entity. He is the personification of the entire universe. He is the first giant and the ancestor to all giants and Gods. He was killed by Odin and his two brothers, Ve and Vili. He gave birth to the Jötnar, primeval beings from his flesh. When Odin and his brothers killed him, Jötnar fled into the rivers and came off him from their father's blood. They scattered across the nine worlds. The nine worlds were formed from Ymir's body. His body became mountains, his blood became sea and oceans. Hair became trees. His eyebrows became Midgard (Earth). Ginnungagap created him.

NARFI . He also was the father of Nótt and was the literal personification of night. He also was the son of Loki. In the Eddic poem called "Lokasenna", he became a wolf and his brother Nari was slaughtered.

MIMIR - One of the oldest and wisest Gods. (origin of the modern English Word Memory) He met his hand after the

Aesir Vs Vanir War. He was a God sent by Odin to negotiate a truce. The Vanir Gods expected him to cheat because of his wisdom. They cut off his head and sent it back to Asgard. They see his body near the Mimisbrunnr well near the deep roots of the world tree, Yggdrasil. The same well where Odin sacrificed one of his eyes for wisdom. Other legends say he preserved his head preserved wit herbs and charms. His head 'lived on' with wisdom and gave Odin advice.

SKADI - Goddess - (pronounced Scottie or also heard SKA) She was associated with winter, skinning and mountains and bowhunting. Some myths say he married the Banir God Njord. Then became the mother of Freyr and Freyja. Scholars also believe the name Scandinavia where these myths came from her name.

BRAGI - God - The husband of the goddess of youth, the God of Poetry. He was the "Bard os Asgard." He seems similar to the 9th-century Bard named Bragi Boddanson. He served in the courts of Ragnar Lodbrok and Bjorn at Hauge. Its unclear if God's myth was referring to the real-life poet or the Gods. Some legends say the real-life bard went to Valhalla and got

"Godhooded" and miraculously became a God for his fame.

IDU - A angelic goddess with long blonde hair. She was a goddess of rejuvenation and eternal youth. Her name translates to The Rejuvenated One. She was the poet's wife above God BRAGI, Idune had fruits called **Epli** that bestowed immortality to those who consumed them. These are described as apples that are said to make Norse Gods immortal. This blonde-haired goddess makes the Norse Gods seem less angelic, less like Gods and more Human. They don't own their immorality to any divine nature but to.... Epli fruit.

HEIMDALL - God - There is no consensus on who his parents were. But some legends say he is a Vanir God. He is best known as a Guardian and Protect of Asgard. He guarded the Bilfrost rainbow bridge. He also had a horn named **GJALLARHORN**. That is used to alert of danger. Strong sense of hearing and eyes to see the danger. Even are comically, "To hear wool growing on sheep or see 100 leagues into the distance."

NJORD - All-father of the Vanir Gods. He was the opposite of Odin who was the father of the Aesir or Asgardian Gods. He

was the father of Freyja and Freyr, the two most famous Vanir deities. God of the sea as well as wealth and fertility. After the Aesir Vs Vanir War. In this war, Both planets, Vanaheim and Asgard, were destroyed, the Marauders destroyed Vanaheim, and Asgard was destroyed because of the Ragnarok. Njord went to Asgards to discuss with the two pantheons. He decided to live there with the Aesir. There, in luxurious halls of Asgard, Njord married **Skadi** who gave birth to Freyja and Freyr. In some myths, the sibling was alive during the Aesir vs Vanir War. Some myths say they were born from a relationship with his own sister. He is known as both a Vanior and an Aesir God. He also is the father of the two most famous Vanir Gods.

FREYR - He was the brother of Freyja, and son of Njord, Freyr was peaceful and a farmer. He is shown as a big brawny man with his pet boar **Gullinborsti**. With the Legends, he is said to ride a chariot pulled by giant boars. He also was one of the two most famous Vanir deities attested to.

FREYJA Goodness - He was the daughter NJORD and a matriarch deity of the Vanir Pantheon. She is the goddess of love, lust, fertility and war. She was the wife of Óðr, the frenzied

one. While peaceful, she didn't hesitate to defend her realm. She also was known as a Goddess of War. She also was the two most famous Vanir deities. She took half of all warriors who died heroically in battle to her heavenly **"Folkvanger."** The other half of the slain warriors joined Odin in Valhalla.

FORSETI - God of Justice and reconciliation. The name translates to: "The presiding One.» Or "President" in modern Icelandic language and Faroese (Pronounced For-wee".) Son of BALDUR and NANNA. He acted as a just judge. As a result, all those who visited him were left reconciled. His justice stands in sharp contrast to TYR, who also sought justice but through war and conflict, not reasoning.

GARM - He was a dog from Hell during Ragnarok. Classic looking werewolf look. He is tied closely with Hel and Ragnarök as a blood-slathered watchdog of Hel's Gate.

TYR - A God of War. He is a favorite among most Germanic Tribes. He was a brave and powerful god who was associated with all the formalities of war and battles, including signing peace treaties. In addition, he worships as the God of justice

and oaths. Most famous for binding the world Fenrir. The wolf thought he was being tricked and attacked. The wolf wanted somebody's and in his jaws if they would put a special chain on him. The wolf saw the trick, could escape, and attacked and bit his hand off. He was killed by Gary, the aforementioned evil werewolf-looking thing.

NORSE PAGANISM

2.1 INTRODUCTION

OOldNorse religion, also known as Norse paganism, is a branch of Germanic religion which originated during the Proto-Norse period. It was replaced by Christianity during the Christianisation of Scandinavia, but is still practised today by a small number of people. Norse religion was polytheistic, involving a belief in various gods and goddesses. These deities were divided into two groups, the Æsir and the Vanir. In some sources, the Vanir were said to have fought an ancient war with the Æsir until they realized they were equally powerful. Among the most widespread deities were the gods Odin and Thor. This world was also populated by various other mythological races, including jötnar, dwarfs, elves, and land-wights. Norse cosmology revolved around a world tree known as Yggdrasil, with various realms existing alongside that of humans, named Midgard. These include multiple afterlife realms, several of which are controlled by a particular deity. Norse society also

contained practitioners of Seiðr, a form of sorcery that some scholars describe as shamanistic. Various forms of burial were conducted, including both inhumation and cremation, typically accompanied by a variety of grave goods.

2.2 RITUALS

There is no one authoritative source for information about Norse paganism and its rituals. Fragments and indirect sources provide a variety of information about pre-Christian rituals in Scandinavia. For example, the mythical sagas tell us a little about the rituals connected to the deities described, but they rarely connect those to the mythology. After the Christianisation of Iceland, these texts were written and it is likely that much knowledge about the rituals had been lost by then. The mythological tales, on the other hand, survived more easily and are probably closer to the original pagan beliefs.

The bodies of the dead were to be cremated together with all their belongings and spread across the ground or at sea, in accordance with other written and archaeological sources on burial customs. Graves are a common archaeological sign of religious activity and provide valuable information about the beliefs of the bereaved. This material can be used to form a more

general understanding of how religious ideas have changed over time. By comparing it to other findings, new perspectives can be formed.

Norse religion was a traditional religion practiced by Norse pagans in Scandinavia before Christianity arrived. Religion was decentralized and had a number of purposes, including the survival and regeneration of society. Local leaders managed the faith on behalf of the community, and the king was the national leader. Prior to Christianity, there was no single term for Norse religion, so it was referred to as nýr sidr (the new custom) and paganism was called forn sidr (ancient custom). Different parts of the country had their own traditions and beliefs, but people could understand each other because of the cultural differences. Sacrifices played an important role in many of the rituals that are known about today, and communal feasting on the meat of sacrificed animals, together with the consumption of beer or mead, was a common part of Scandinavian calendar festivals. In everyday practice, other foodstuffs like grains were more likely to have been used instead. The purpose of these sacrifices was to ensure fertility and growth, but they could also be used to deal with sudden crises or transitions. After Christianisation, the possession of such figures was banned and severely punished.

Several sources from different periods mention chariots being used in fertility rituals across Scandinavia.

2.3 WORSHIP OF GODS

Recentresearch suggests that the communal festivals held throughout large regions of a population were not as important as the more local celebrations that took place among individual members of that population.

Though they were written in a later Christian era, the Icelandic sagas are of great significance as sources to everyday religion. Even whilst the Christian have an impact on is taken into account, they draw a photo of faith intently tied to the cycle of the 12 months and the social hierarchy of society. In Iceland, the neighborhood secular chief had the name of gothi, which at the start supposed priest however withinside the Middle Ages changed into a time period for a neighborhood secular chief.

Ceremonial communal meals in connection with the blót sacrifice are mentioned in several sources and are thus some of the most described rituals. Masked dancers, music, and making

a song can also additionally were not unusualplace components of those feasts. As in different pre-Christian Germanic societies, however in evaluation to the later state of affairs beneathneath Christianity, there has been no magnificence of priests: all and sundry should carry out sacrifices and different religion acts. However, not unusualplace cultural norms intended that it become typically the character with the very best repute and the best authority (the top of the own circle of relatives or the chief of the village) who led the rituals. The reassets suggest that sacrifices for fertility, a secure journey, an extended life, wealth. Were a natural and fully integrated part of daily life in Scandinavian society, as in almost all other pre-modern societies across the world.

2.4 FAITHS, STATUES AND IMAGES

Manysources mention statues of pagan gods, which are commonly described as wooden staves with faces carved on top. Ahmad ibn Fadlan writes approximately such poles in his description of a Scandinavian sacrifice on the Volga. This account indicates that the statues might also additionally have a connection to mythology, however it's miles not possible to decipher it. No such big statues from the Viking Age have been found, only small figures and amulets. This may be because larger statues were deliberately destroyed after Christianity became the dominant religion. After Christianisation, the possession of such figures was banned and severely punished. Many accounts of missionaries describe the destruction of pagan idols as a major victory, symbolising the strength of the Christian god over the weak, "devilish" native gods. The sagas also mention small figures that can be kept in a purse.

These figures are known from archaeological findings across Scandinavia, including hammer-shaped jewelry, golden men or figures of gods. It is possible that this motif can be traced back to processions from the Bronze Age.

2.5 HUMAN SACRIFICE

There has been much disagreement about whether human sacrifice was practised in Scandinavia. Numerous discoveries of bog bodies and evidence of sacrifices of prisoners of war from the Pre-Roman Iron Age show that such killings were not uncommon in Northern Europe in the period before the Viking Age. Additionally, some findings from the Viking Age can be interpreted as evidence of human sacrifice, including children as young as four years old. Some sagas mention human sacrifice at temples, as does Adam of Bremen. Commanders could consecrate the enemy warriors to Odin using their spears, thus war was ritualised and made sacral. Violence became part of each day existence withinside the Viking Age and took on a non secular that means like different activities. It is possibly that human sacrifice happened throughout the Viking Age however it isn't clean that it became a part of not unusualplace public non secular practise. Instead it became most effective practised in reference to strugglefare and in instances of crisis.

VIKINGS AGE

3.1 INTRODUCTION

TheVikings lived on the fat of the land and liked to pillage every now and then. The etymology of the word in Old Norse translates to "Pirate Raid." They were conquerors, harvesters, worshipers, lovers, and sometimes barbarians of Dark Ages brutality. The term Viking is not an ethnic or a regional term. There are also Irish and Slavic Vikings. The Viking period is dated from 790 to 1066 AD and the age commenced with the attack on the Holy Island of Lindisfarne. However, there would be squashes is a little bit before this state and explorations after, but this general is the documented date of the Age of Vikings.

In the early settlement period, many early 8th Century pioneers were of mixed Celtic marriages. Anthropologists and scholars believe European Slavs were also part of the first Viking settlers in Scandinavia and Iceland. These people would soon conquer the world for five hundred years by the iron axe and the innovative mind.

The Vikings came into prominence at the very end of the Vendel

Period. Which a period from the early migration times of 550 to 790 AD and would dominate global affairs for five hundred years through ingenuity and brutality.

They were pantheistic, believing the universe and god are connected. They believed the All Mighty and the cosmos were interwoven like sword and a shield. Rather than some man in the clouds of Christian beliefs, it is more about the limitless universe as a reflection of a deity. They were also polytheistic, which means they believed and worshipped many gods. Odin, Thor or Freya. They believed in animals and spiritual essence and were, thereby, Animists. The landscapes once full of forest wood were laid bear within fifty years. Part of it would be for timber, but the other part would be for animal grazing. The Vikings come from modern-day Scandaiviana and had bitter clan rivalries. They had tremendous skill with the axe and even throwing it. They would ride in longships devised to cross the sprawling sea.

Examples of clans:

Wægmunding, in Beowulf.

Ylfing or Wulfing in Beowulf and Norse Sagas.

Scylfing (Yngling)

Skjöldung (Scylding)

Völsung

They were first lowly Scandinavian farmers and then developed brilliant shipwrights skills. In most farms, a boat yard was devised on traditions going back 100s of years. These boats were the pinnacle of innovation were known as Drakeskip or Dragonships. They were made to instill fear in the enemy as they approach for raids. The angular design of the ship shaped a bitch like a bullhorn, allows for remarkable flex on the ship axis. These innovative readerships would change history.

In order to find the built ideal vessel with their craftsmanship, they would look for curved branches that would match the boat they are trying to construct. Sometimes they would use oak to build their ships, but other times it would be pine. Through the long, laborious day, they would use their finely sharpened axes and take these large planks of wood to the harbors. There, the masterful boat builders would use their pioneering skills would construct boats that with seaworthy but also able to be pulled crossed land for invasions. Each of those boats would be built using the Clinker Technique, where the edges of the rounded interior of the ship overlap. Viking Woman would weld the mighty sails known as the 'dragon's

wing.' When a great big wave comes splashing in the boat can flex to the motion of the water and reduce the impact. The subtle flexibility of the construction of the hull also makes it more agile on the sea. So swift on the scholars would guess their ships could go as fast as twenty knots, something only modern sailing boats would compete with. They were quickly simply the perfect ocean-going vessel for raiding or exploring uncharted lands.

Simply put, they could outmaneuver rival ships. They were ahead of their time with their inventive, industrious minds. Their shipbuilding would get them to conquer the world. So the land became depleted of resources, and the sea fairy men learned more about the world. They sought virgin lands.

All across the highness, they would use advanced maritime naval skills. They would create sun compasses and use the very shadow on indention lines to navigate. Other things they were supremely skillful with were astronomical navigation for seafaring. They would use the stars to guide them on the open ocean and also knew the teachings of the 6th century Ancient greek Pythagoras, the world was round. They were sometimes using the Polar Star. They could use the moon and the time of the season to ensure how the sea would

be and navigation accordingly. Though, and the story of Leif Erikson would tell, they still would occasionally get lost as sea and end up in unfamiliar lands. It's estimated using modern-day navigation GPS, the Vikings knowledge of the sea was only off by 2% to 4%. They were well-versed in the century ancient greek Ptolemy geography knowledge. The ambition was in their blood.

In an area known as Sweden, they would mont their boats and become renowned seafarers. Their boots would travel all along Europe to the Boeing and the Volga. Not always warriors and plunderers were they also civil and respectful of the cultures. These early Norsemen would trade all around the Baltic sea, Caspian and black sea. The ships would be full of amber, eiderdown, salt, livestock, and precious metals would be some of the methods of trade. One of the signature things they would trade, were animal fur, feathers, whalebone, falcons, ivory, reindeer antler and even walrus. In distant empires and corners of the globe, kings, queens, princes and sultans would be using skins that were traded from Vikings. Other things of more nefarious nature that they would sell, human enslaved people purloined in their warpaths. The German town of Hedeby was a prime location for human trade. The people would call them

"The Rus," and they would rule a landscape that bears their name known as Russia. The Land the Rus controlled was a sprawling region just about stretching as far as the U.S.S.R. did. They had a capital known as Kyiv, currently Ukraine's capital. There became known for their resourcefulness and integrity in the battlefield. They tried to truce and take control of the Byzantine Empire. Emperor Basil II, would make them the hired personalty for his army. These mercenaries were called Varangians. Perhaps, to become a natural partner and ally with them rather than ever try to battle with the blades of the Viking warriors again. They would get furs and grades from their Slavic slaves, sometimes with the Arabs in the region.

To enlighten courage, communicate and immortalize the fallen, and they would use Runes. There are two runic languages, the Elder Futhark and the Younger Futhark (more on Chapter Fifteen).

They would trade with any culture and were not always brutal raiders but rather a culture of proud men and women that worshiped many gods but lived in the harsh reality of the dark ages. There was no police to control the laws, pillagers, rapers, murderers, thieves, or any accused malefactor. Therefore, clan

members tribes formed something called **Thing.** Each Viking Community would have a proto-court public meeting place where these marauders could settle issues from family squabbles to train disputes with duals. The Law Speaker with communicate the law completely by his own memory, and not any written down law. This methodology partly contributes to why so many North Myths were contradictory or scatterbrained. The usage of word of mouth and instead of writing. Then in this place called Thing, the chieftain ruled were the way of the land and where the judge, jury, and executioners. They had clans that would wage war with one another, sometimes off of petty scrimmages and other times off of expanding the land in the fertile lands of Scandinavia. They live by the axe, and they sometimes die by the axe.   The Spaniards were looking for gold. The Vikings factions were looking for Silver. Europe was there for the taking. The Vikings factions, we're looking for Silver. Europe was there for the taking.

3.2 EQUIPMENT

BOATS

The Vikings were seafaring people who took to the water like a herring. From ship burials to bloody invasions to discovering Newfoundland, ships were a crucial ingredient to the identity of the Vikings as much as the battle axe and some good ale. Many of them were grateful on water and could be

carried inland for warfare. Within shadow water or the deep abyss of the Atlantic, their unique structure and engineering prowess would help them annihilate their foes and explore and embark on voyages to explore the furthest reaches of the sea.

Drakeskip or **Dragonships,** more commonly known by the name **Drakkar** due to a French transcription error, the most infamous that is depicted often in Viking culture throughout centuries. Part of their predatory nature would be conveyed by their menacing boats. The gray-brown Viking ships were state of the art and revolutionary, were marine vessels of usually striped crimson and white sails. The longship's unique structure used in Scandinavia from the Viking Age throughout the Middle Ages. Viking boats varied broadly depending on voyage and cargo. The boats had low draft and could be carried by hand for raiding. A technology marvel for the medieval period. They were after plunger with bloodthirsty barbarism for their own survival.

Knarr - These run of the mill sailing ships had about 900 feet of storage and were the freighters for trade. The biggest ones like this were able to store as much as 40 tons in wooden barrels

and love stock and people.

Faering or dinghies - For short travel. They would be supporting ships that would follow the larger ones. One of the most known things they would do is Pyre Burial. A ceremony where they would put the dead into a boat filled with wood and then set the boat ablaze. But it with a torch or by archers. The Vikings believed the bodies turned to ash helped them reach the afterlife of Valhalla. A place of the Gods that is quintessential heaven. The ship burials were used with other cultures around the globe. But it was widely used among Germanic peoples with the Vikings Rule.

WEAPONS

Norsemen had a strong penchant for weaponry. Throughout history, Vikings are depicted as Axe and sword-welding savages with horns, hats and mangled teeth, and fierce eyes. Whilst they had a fierce arsenal of weapons to get in tactical advantage and not always thoughtless barbarians. They were industrious craftsmen of sometimes elegant tools of bloodshed or intimation.

The early Norseman had many weapons at their disposal, quick to protect themselves. Historians believe that some slept with their weapons in their hands to be at ready at any moment. They would have battle axes, single-handed swords or two-handed single-handed larger Swords, spears, bows, and something called a Viking Seax, which is a large dagger good for cutting a throat and chopping pork. Many of these weapons would be used for tactical advantage on the battlefield.

The weapons of the Norsemen were more than just weapons of war for bloodbaths, and they were, at times, sacred like a gift from Thor. There is some archaeological data that suggests that Vikings would "kill" their swords. It was a method of bending the blades so they would be unusable in a ritualistic fashion. Essentially, it was like retiring a weapon, perhaps when a warrior died or gave off his spilling blood ways of old. Other things, it would render the weapon useless, for any grave robber would want to purloin the blade and make a mint. Many of the blades would be found at Viking burial sites, with these deceased blades rendered useless. Just as the Vikings sometimes had an unusual brutal process for people with the funeral pyre, they would sometimes be even unusual with their treatment of weapons of

war. Here are some highlights of Scandinavian weaponry there were used many millennia ago and still today.

AXES

Axes were cheap multipurpose wrought iron weapons that would both chop down timber and also chop a man in half. These are the most run-of-the-mill weapon of Norsemen, though some could decorate their sword with Celtic lettering all over the blade. Battle axes and common axes were distinguishable, though in size and sharpness, and edges. The Vikings would, at times, give names to their weapons like it was cherished loved one. The feelings of sentimentality toward a weapon were common. The most famous Axe in Norse history was named "Hel" with one single L. That distinguishing spelling corn sides with the Goddess of Death. This famous Axe was first owned by Olav Haraldsson. Then it was inherited by his son The, King Magnus of Norway and Denmark. According to Prose Edda, Axe would be named after female jötnar or in laymen's terms, female trolls. It said that Poorer men would have little other in

their procession but this and a shield. For a Common Norsemen, a study axe would be a lifesaver.

VIKING SWORDS (also a Carolingian sword)

These shoulder companions were for Norsemen of mostly only high pedigree. Swords required Swordsmiths, and to fashion and temper the blade perfectly required both ingenuity and money. One of the logical reasons is that iron was a much sought-after thing within Scandinavia. Thus, finding some to fashion a weapon was scarce. Thereby, this is not the common weapon for the common Norse.

One of the more famous Viking swords, The Sæbø sword, was found in the 1800s in Norway's district in Western Sogn. This blade, like many others, has its notable inscription on the blade and runic letters on it. Over the years, Vikings would squire understanding of the Roman alphabet and use those letters on their mighty blades too. The sword, sometimes called the Carolingian Sword, was the quintessential weapon of the Norseman in leading to the social elite. They also communicated masculinity in a bond with one's family or a king. Each sword was around ninety Centimeters in length.

Within Norse Mythology, The God of War, Freyr was known for his great sword to slew his adversaries. The tale spoken about said that Frayr had forsaken his sore in a way to her love. It said he traded his sword got he giant Skírnir for the marriage to the Jötunn, the giant named Gerðr. That would be his pathway to his own demise. For within that climatic battle, Ragnarok, he would not have his famous Claymore blade and would be killed by the fire giant known as Surt. Perhaps this is a morality tale for the ages, if a Viking does not have his weapon at hand to slew any enemy, perhaps he will meet his bitter end like the Freyr.

SPEAR

The most attested-to spear in all of Norse Mythology would be the Gungnir. This Odin's sacred weapon was made by the Sons of Ivaldi and would; besides his missing eye, the long medal blade would be one of the signature characteristics of the Allfather. This, like the Axe, would be a very conventional long-killing tool on the battlefield. Even peasants would fashion a spear out of wood or tempered metal. Because they are commonplace, the metal would be of inferior quality to that of a sword. Just like other weapons, the Norsemen considered spears sacred, and

they would throw their spears at any enemies for a lethal strike. But unlike Odin's spear, which would not miss its target, it was a mortal's weapon and for the common Viking in need. The Pagan God Odin would say this to remind his warriors, "Don't leave your weapons lying about behind your back in a field; you never know when you may need all of sudden your spear."

BOW AND ARROW

Norsemen could also be precision tacticians on the battlefield and could use bows and arrows to gain advantage points. Though would be used not just for hunting men but for poaching games in the wilderness for their families. Just like the aforementioned weapons, they could be adorned with Latin lettering or runes from the elder futhark or the young futhark. These were purely utilitarian, and we're not really a prize whirly weapon as they were easy to break down when the string snapped. This bend would with string was not something you hang all a wall like a magnificent sword but treat it more hand me down thing of little ceremonial value.

VIKING SEAX/KNIFE

If you get a tap on her shoulder from behind by a Viking, you
may get stabbed with one of these using the element of surprise.
The Seax was the knife of the longest creed that would be as
long as sixty cementers one. Most of them had a sharp angled
from the part back to the topmost point. They also would work
in conjunction who a Viking who had a sword. The blades were
used as a second-hand weapon or a stealth weapon for surprise
attacking a foe. The word Seax translates to "Knife." Virtually
every Viking had a dagger with them to cut at the throat or chop
sinews of meat. They would be fastened inside of the *cabbard*,
the holder and dangle in horizontal fashioned long a Norsemen's
belt.

It was a companioned weapon, a mighty claymore, an axe, or a
trusty spear. From the 7th century onward, the blade became
more of an angled tool in a C shape and less of a straight vertical
blade. It is a perfect, travel-ready, killing instrument.

HELMETS

Within many of the Viking Sage Sagas, there are reports that

swords would swing right through those weak helmets and leave warriors with a mighty head wound or worst. One of the big questions from scholars is how effective helmets were in real-world battlefields with hit with a claymore or an arrow. The reason is they were usually fabricated out of a weaker grade of iron called bog iron. So the other question is if the helmets were merely a status signal and not considered any protective Head ornament. Just like the claymore, the sword theorized that the higher class was the one dawning that iron on their Head. The poorer or more common warrior might have been dawning woolen hats or Frisian hats.

There also are no archaeological findings of a Viking helmet with horns. The helmets were used to protect their heads in battle from a mighty sly strike or a precision arrow, and they are not deemed exactly decorative. One would imagine horns on either side would be like a farce in the real-world life-or-death skirmish.

From research, only five fully intact Viking helmets that ever been found. So their nature of them is still cloaked in shadow to this day. Some of them were doctrine in design with angular

shapes communicating their predatory nature in war. Others were painted in various colors to give them more of a ceremonial depiction or for brute intimidation of an enemy.

SHIELDS

If a Viking was going to sack a town, they needed an axe or sword, and then a good shield. The were savvy tacticians and knew of the various methods in combat to use them to save warriors' life in the heat of battle. They also were good use to wart off a barrage of lethal arrows or a swing from an Axe or Sword.

CHAINMAIL

Chainmail was a common protective medal shirt within Iron Age and the Middle Ages. If you were a Viking of higher status, perhaps you could afford the quintessential weapon, the sword; there is a chance you could afford chainmail. These would be small metal rings that were linked and could protect your torso from a deadly strike. Going waist-length or even as far as around your Head, they could be a mighty defensive tool if one is looking to sack a Kingdom.

FOOD

When the Vikings were not plundering, they had to fill their bellies with sustenance. Due to the fact they were from a Northern climate, they would eat food that would be consistent with that sometimes cold region where they were white-knuckling through the hardships. Like their religion of Norse Paganism, things were not written in a cookbook fashioned but more word of mouth. They would eat using utensils like spoons and forks. The average day of the life of a Norsemen was to have two meals, morning and night.

When the Vikings first got out of bed for their breakfast meal, they would go to their cauldron and pour some dagmál (day meal) from yesterday's bread. Their rest of the Norsemen or Norsewoman's day's dietconsisted of high-protein meals from cows, lambs, fish, eggs, chickens, and pigs and meals with a large variety of vegetables. These meals were called náttmál", or (night meal).

Sometimes there would be meat stew and nuts with sweetened honey within them too. The fire used to cook their food was called a máleldr or "meal-fire." But as the Vikings evolved

and their rule in the world started to dwindle, they started to assimilate into other cultures and learn their cuisines.

3.3 WHERE DID THE VIKINGS GO?

W herethey were once Pagan warriors, they slowly became domesticated Christians into a slowly dwindling anarchy warpath of the globe. With their mindset of chaos

fading, their blades dulling, Pagan traditions dwindling, so did the Viking culture. Normandy became land of the Normans, Russia was land of the Russian. The story of precisely how the Vikings became Christians is convoluted and piecemeal with a lot of moving pieces and not just bloodbaths. Christianity and Paganism co-excited for many years incorporating elements of one another A Treaty of Wedmore was signed in 878 between. The treaty bound the Viking leader Guthrum to accept Christianity, with Alfred the Great, the King of the West Saxons from 871 – c. 886, offering peace in return. Recognized Guthrum as the ruler of East Anglia. Whatever the Vikings' reasons for converting at the time, the result was that by the end of the Viking Age, most of Scandinavia had converted to Christianity. By the 12th century Sweden was predominately Christian as was the rest of Scandinavia. Many Vikings didn't want to abandoned the heathen traditions. Some of those would be eating horses and infanticide or brutal tradition like the Pyre Burial. But they would make a pact with Norway, that Christendom was soon come by the wishes of King Olaf Tryggvason. Another reason why things started fade for the Norsemen, the climate started to change in Greenland and farming got more arduous.

The warpath and conquest came to an end partly because of Christianity made them more civil through the teachings of Jesus, and also got them to assimilate into other cultures through the millennia. The Norse Pagan religion had been relegated to the realm of myths and legends an archaeologist began to excavate bones from Greenland to find out the mystery of where the Norse People went. They believe it was ecological and social economic ramifications that factor into the reason why there are no more Norseman in Greenland. It is theorized, the early Norsemen were overgrazing their animals and rapid deforestation of the landscape. The jury is still out by historians if they were the catalyst of all those or it was just natural progression of Greenland. The soil erosion was simply not the fertile place it once was with the early settlements. They just didn't have a good place to call home.

One of their primary places for living was becoming a problematic place to live and they thought to merge into other cultures around the globe or parish of starvation. The environment was colder in Greenland and was now turning closer to an Ice Land. Fjords, rising lands on either side of ships, were being barcoded by ice and simply getting delivery of food and timber was being more scarce from Labrador

and Norway. The Norsemen of Greenland were becoming landlocked and marooned without ships. Archaeological evidence says that they were in such dire straits they were consuming 'bone soup'. Meaning, soup made of finely grinned down bone. Further examination reveals they were eating their dogs, something historical evidence says they did not do. However, there is only theories why the Norse left Greenland but a guest guesstimate would would be a various factors and the change of the environmental conditions would play a heavy part into that. It's inconclusive what exactly was the problem why the left. The final day for the Norsemen in Greenland were nevertheless harsh and merciless. Overgrazing or overforesting or not, science data reveals things were getting steadily more dire by the day in Greenland many millennia ago.

As the heathens became Christians, things were starting to change around the globe. Ragnarok never came or them but Christianity, overgrazing, deforestation and bitter chill of environmental changes did. The Viking-age faded out into history and was at an end. Though they are descendants from Vikings, Today Scandinavians are some most peaceful people the world. They did a world's favorite to get it out of their system. May these fearsome warriors rest in peace.

KINGS AND BATTLES

4.1 RAGNAR LOTHBROK

H is life and death have been clocked in the ambiguity of time and word-of-mouth legend. Ragnar, like Ragnarok, was a name synonymous with a warpath. Viking Leader **Ragnar Lothbrok (Loðbrók)** was perhaps the most infamous Viking for his lust for equal measures, conquests, and carnage. He has been Immortalized for millenniums all across ligature and entrainment. He could be, quite simply, the archetypal depiction of a Viking. The 13th-century *Tale of Ragnar Lodbrok*, a legendary Icelandic saga, cryptic poems, and carvings on a stone called epigraphics would uncloak the mystery of this mythic man. He is known as a legendary barbarian of Vikings lore and sought to pillage Holy Roman Empire. He was the first to attack the British Isles and one of the chief architects of the warpath that began the age of the Vikings.

What scholars construed from various sources, Sagas and

legends as he was born in Scandinavia. He was the son of **King of Sweden Sigurd Ring**. The litany of reasons is his penchant for warfare, his cold-bloodedness, his present of mind for strategy, and his unwavering desire for imperialism. It is believed he had three sons **Halfdan**, **Inwaer** (Ivar the Boneless), and **Hubba** (Ubbe). There are also theories that he could be a couple of people combined into one. Historians do know that his sons are indeed real flesh and blood people with documented evidence. Like many historians would agree, a true ironclad understanding of Ragnar would be impassive as so much of him longs to the hands of time. His background comes from Icelandic and has mythical power properties that sound a bit like something of Prose Edda.

The tale goes of his formidable years, and the Young Ragnar took a blade to a giant brood of snakes that guarded the abode of the Geatish jarl Herrauð's daughter **Thora Borgarhjort**. The Legends about his almost mythical backstory could be an exaggeration. But in the ancient text, it is inscribed he gutted gargantuan venomous snakes in cold blood to win a woman's heart. Then devised armor and including breachers out of animal hide rolled said. Thus earning her affection for the woman who would be become his wife. At that same time, he would get the

nickname of Ragnar, "Hairy Breeches." He would go on to be the most prominent Viking in history.

According to *Sögubrot*, an ancient Icelandic text, he was even fare of faced and handsome. His militia of armed, axed, ferocious warriors were known as the Great Heathen Army. One of the more barbaric things the Vikings were known to do was the Blood Eagle, a form of torture where ribs were removed and then contorted and shaped like an eagle. The middle ages were just as inky black as the dark ages.

With a sea spawning one hundred and twenty longships, and ten thousand Great Heathen warriors, the cutthroat Ragnar Lothbrok and his crew launched a blitzkrieg attack. They attacked the unassuming monks in a blindsided attack. In an undocumented time, perhaps under the cloak of night, he assailed the Holy Island of Lindisfarne with a vengeance. Pillage, plunder, kidnap, do a Blood Eagle or two, and every atrocity you can think of between. By the waters, they rampaged with their dragon ships, axes, swords, and throat-cutting tiny Seax blades. He and his ruffians with axes and shields would conquer with little regard for humanity the once sacred countryside.

The onslaught on the Siege of Paris came in 845 AD. Then he launched an incursion on Paris's motherland by Dragon ship,

grit, and axe. The event was known as the Siege of Paris (885–886). This was the first of two making Viking Raids during this time. Ragnar's men decimated the French's advancing force on the Seine River. He would later withdraw his forces after Frankish King Charles the Bald paid him a handsome amount of money. This went on for decades along the Seine and Loire Rivers. The Vikings conquer all in their path unhindered. It had the opposite effect. The onslaught on Northern Europe went onward. Between 790 and 1100 AD, Vikings followed every major river or water route from Scandinavia into Europe and England. King Aella of Northumbria, the **King Of Anglo-Sexon** England, would capture him, and he would meet a gruesome end fitting of his formidable mythological years.

The bound and ensnared Viking Ragnar was thereby sentenced to death or murder, mayhem raiding homes. At the behest of somebody who knew of his backstory tied to snakes, or perhaps just a make-believe writer's imagination through the millenniums, his judgment would be fitting of his life saga. Thereby he would meet his end by capital punishment and into a slithering and sapping snake pit. The infamous Viking would be thrown in a pit for numerous atrocities in the countryside. As the snakes dug into his flesh, the venom coursed into his

bloodstream. His eyes would roll up in his head, and his rampaging spirit would depart him under the veil of starlight. The Viking Hero Ragnar Lothbrok would soon come to the gates of Valhalla. Through folkloric, Sagas, modern-day programming, and literature, he would be enshrined into's people's psyche as the most notorious but also legendary Viking that ever lived. It was at the end of his life when the age of the Vikings seemed everlasting and indestructible.

4.2 ERIK THE RED

T heMost Famous Viking was known for his flaming red hair and tempestuous attitude, and discovery of a very piece of land. Eric The Red was born c. 950 in Jæren, Norway. His brithname wasn Erik Thorvaldsson. Like many legendary Norsemen of Legends, not much is known about early life. One thing that he knows is his father tilled the earth and was a farmer named Thorvald Asvaldsson. He was found guilty of murder. Under the reign of King Haakon the Good, Erik The Red's blood-spilling father was banished from Norway and lost all his land. The Thorvaldsson Family relocated to Iceland. They resettled in the Northwestern Part of the Island of an area called Hornstrandir. At the age of 12, Norse Boys were required to help with farming. Two years after moving there, everybody saw him as a grown man, but he would be known to have a flaming temper. The harsh elements of the land toughened him, and he started to take after his father in mannerisms. After his father died, he married the daughter of a wealthy family known

as the Thjodhild Jörundsdóttir. They moved to Haukadalur and named their farm Eiriksstadir. Four of their five children would live into adulthood and would make their way into history.

Within that time, it was typical for Norsemen to own slaves, or in Norsemen Term's *Surfs* or *Thralls*. Some of the slaves trigger a landslide and then crush his neighbor Valthjol's house. Eric did not have a great relationship with his neighbors. One of Valthjol's clansmen, named Eyiolf the Foul, killed Erik's thralls. Eric was none-too-pleased. He killed Eyiolf and another man named Holmgang-Hrafn. As Eric killed a fellow Norsemen, like his father, he was forced to move from his homestead. He moved to an Icelandic farmland called Oxney and rebuilt his home. Norseman was used to rebuilding their homes as mold would creep in. They would not replace the wooden beams of the house called the Setstokkr.

They would have elaborate carvings and sometimes be adorned with runes for mythical properties. His father kept his father's Setstokkr he bought with him from Norway. Though historians are not all convinced, this framework was indeed his father's or not. As he rebuilt his home, he had a guest named Thorgest.

He refused to return his father's Setstokkr. So, Eric took it by force and got it back. He knew they would counterattack and Erik set up an ambush of Thorgust's clan. Erik killed two of Thorgest's sons. Once again, Erik the Red was guilty of murder and banished from Iceland entirely. He used his persuasive skills to keep his own land in his possession and agreed to be in exile for three years.

This proved that Erik has veracity for languages just as much for combat. During his time of being banished, he spent his time along the ocean with his valiant crew. In 982, he set sail from Snaefellsjokull and on a voyage to explore a landmass westward through the fog-entrenched sea. It is within this time frame that Erik saw the ice-embedded shoreline. He needed to think of a good name that would market the island by word of mouth to increase the population and in the same breath, Erik's notoriety. Thus, he named it "Greenland." Historians believe he named this part glacial and part lush green island because the land was partially covered in ice it so it was more appealing to settlers. Norsemen were mostly farmers, to the idea of fertile Green land was a tantalizing prospect to consider elsewhere. He and his gallant men sailed to the western side of the island

before they found a place to land a ship. He would spend three years in exile and explore vast new Scandinavian settlement countryside throughout the seasons. Eric reconnaissance of the island revealed it wasn't the perfect land, the soil was fertile and ripe for growth. There would be no inhabitants, and Eric took lightning to it due to his tempestuous attitude.

Their first winter was spent on an island they called Eriskay. When the thaw came, they sailed up a rising rocky land on either side called a fjord. They would form a settlement on a place aptly named *Eriksford*. During the second winter, they dwelled in an encampment called Eriksholmar. Most of the places he visited he merely named after himself. Within Iceland, his family would be attending to his farm and waiting for his voyage home. Eric decided when his three years were up he would abandon Iceland and live there with his family. He convened around 500 other people to live there with him. The method of how he convened 500 people to leave their homes to live somewhere without any civilization remains a mystery. No doubt, his persuasive verbal skills helped pull off that. Others may have had the enthusiasm to be one of the first to colonize the land. Twenty-five ships with men, women, and children disembarking set sail for Greenland.

A little over half of the ships made their way to the largest, most gargantuan island in the world, with many during back due to the arduous journey, blown off course, and perhaps second guessing.

There would be two colonies set up on the island. The first is Qaqortaq, which is near the current capital of Greenland Nuuk. The houses that were built were in the traditional Longhouse style. Within Greenland, trees are a rare commodity, saw the houses were built out of stone. Erik constructed his new home at the head of Eriksford and was the chief of the settlement. In order for the growth of the island, Greenlanders traded various things with Norwegians and Icelandic various furs. Polar bear fur, caribou skins, arctic fox furs, and seal pelts were things that helped build the island's prosperity. These are things that could be traded for timber, rare things for Greelanders. One of the more mythological things the people of Greenland would sell would be Unicorn horns. Even though there was no such thing as Unicorns, it was a thing of Fantasy and legend as much as a flaming dragon, and there was such a thing as a medium-sized whale called Narwhal. Thing things inhabited the Greenland waters, and their tusks could be petals off as unicorn horns for

a high sum of money. Erik the Red would live on his years in relative peace and tranquility. They would be no more reports of murder mayhem for the man with the flaming red hair. But one of his sons would soon become world famous for what he would discover along the high seas on a voyage into the unknown.

4.3 LEIF ERIKSON, ERIK THE RED AND VIKING COLONIZATION

Leif Erikson, was a legendary Viking explorer and also known as Leif the Lucky. He also was the son of Erik The Red. Many explorers of the Vikings era had nicknames or "Cognomens" and this one was fitting of him. His perilous voyages upon the sea were not that of luck but more of conviction and courage. Lief was one of history's forgotten explorers and discovered Northern America, Known as Vínland (Wine Land). The Vikings were there 500 years before Columbus. The two main sources that chronicle the Viking's explorations of North America. These two Icelandic Legends are known as *The Saga Of Erik The Red* and *The Saga of the Greenlanders*. Both of these were written about 250 years after the settlement of

Greenland. Both of these sagas are somewhat cryptic in what they say and are open to scholarly interpretation. When using archaeological evidence of these voyages, skeletons were found buried deep in Finland. one can remove the fogginess of Viking history and conclude these mythical sagas could be a historical reality of Norse Explorers.

Lief Erikson came from a bloodline of explorers. To the best guess of scholars, he was born in Iceland in 970 but lived in Greenland. He was a middle child, and had two brothers. Thorvard, and Thorstein and a sister named Freydis. He was described as wise, strong, considerate and with striking Norse looks. When he was a child, who would watch the ships come in and listen to the stories of men and their adventures on the high sea. He has raised me a slave named Threiker. (Thryiker) was captured by Erik The Red in a raid in Germany. The Slave was put in charge of tutoring Leif. The Slave taught him everything from reading and writing runes and the Celtic and Russian languages also about trade, religion, and the old Sagas and weapons.

The reason why this Slave indoctrinated Leif on the ways of

the world was quite simple: his father was the legendary Erik The Red, Erik Thorvalsson, A Pagan Chieftain. His father was a well-known explorer who founded the new Norse Colonies in Greenland to great notoriety. His father was expelled from his home in Iceland for being convicted of murder. His distant relative was Naddodd The Viking when he was blown off course in 861. Thus, relative of Leif Erikson and his father was credited for discovering Ice Land. Leif came from a family of Norse Explorers. When Leif sat around a candle-lit table in his father's castle, he met a lustrous woman. In the year 999, he married a woman named Thorgunna.

They would have a kid named Thorkell. He would set sail for Norway and be greeted by many people. He was taken to King Olaf Tryggvason's Castle. He was on his last year of his reign, and enthusiastically wanted to meet this brave Viking. He knew Lief's father very well and wanted him to stay in Norway. Leif Erikson enjoyed Norway and felt lethargic about going back home. He was part of the King's inner circle and was treated like royalty. One time, he was playing chess with King Olaf Tryggvason and he told how he used to worship the old Heathen Gods of the bygone age. Then a plague came to Norway and he had an epiphany of a new deity to worship. He would go

into detail about the Black Death, and the Bubonic Plague that historians in the aftermath estimated killed either one-third or two-thirds of the Norwegian population. The King told of how the Old Gods of Thor and Odin were fading from their world and then started to learn the ways of the bible and to worship Jesus. Leif had no loyalty to the old Pagan God's of Odin and Thor. It was then Soon thereafter, he was baptized along with umpteen thousands of people of the country. The Black Death started to fade, and the death doll dwindled. Leif went on his voyage back home with a priest from the king. He then proselytized the religion across Greenland, and he spread the word of this carpenter named Jesus Christ. They saw Christianity as a way to unite the clans. Thus, being able to govern them for the betterment of Viking society.

The King asked Leif to Christianize Greenland in order to squash rivalries between clans. At the dawn of the 11th century, 200 years after the rampage on Lindisfarne and its monasteries, the Norse People had no King and fought with one another. The New Religion was a way to reunite. The Pagan Vikings were frightened to give up their Gods. They were Christian missionaries that tried to convert people, but they were skeptical. Then they

decided to go into a test with Pagan Gods, and berserkers, the representative of the Pagan gods. This man was a little bit dragged. And the test was if one of the representatives could pass through a Christian fire, the religion would be legitimate. Or if he could pass through a Pagan fire, that would be the legitimate religion. The berserker passed easily through the fire made by the Pagans. He could not get through the fire made by the Christians. Everybody around those fires saw that Christianity was the correct religion because the berserker could not pass through the fire. Then it was decided what allegiances to what Faith would be and therefore embrace the monotheistic ideas of Christianity of one God. One of the stories in the Sagas starts with Lief in Greenland. There is debate if how accurate these tales on the high seas are or if they are looking to create a myth for the ages. Archaeological evidence of North America would cooperate with many of these tales from the Icelandic Sagas. Without a shed of doubt, the stories are not completely accurate by way of oral storytelling of this area rather than putting into text, which occurs over two hundred years later.

The story described in the Sagas tell of young Viking Lief Erikson was on the shoreline watching boats and saw an old

merchant ship. It belonged to explorer Bajani Herjólfsson and traveled from Iceland to Greenland. Bajani Herjólfsson wanted to visit Erik The Red, Leif's father. His father had been gone for a year or more, and he had been banished from his country for murder. Leif Erikson and Bajani sat down at a table with a tale to tell. He told the young Lief of the voyage he had. The Young Leif followed Bajani Herjólfsson to a hall in Greenland and told him of a voyage he had. Bajani told him how mist covered the North Star and was confused about his direction on the sea. Along the Atlantic waters, Bajani and his valiant crew sailed for many days through the arduous sea. Late in the summer, Bajani said he spotted land that was not Greenland as there were no coastal glaciers. Along the sandy shoreline, he saw lush green trees but didn't want to stay there as winter was coming in a quarter season. As his exploratory adventure ended, Bajani went back to Greenland during the winter season to meet Leif and his father, The King. According to Saga of the Greenlanders (Grænlendinga saga), it is believed Bajani Herjólfsson was the first European to spot North America to the naked eye.

Like a lightning bolt from Thor hit them, Leif Erikson was galvanized with dreams of explorations. Lief the Lucky was

inspired by Bajani's adventure and discovery of a New World and wanted to make a name for himself doing the same. The Young Viking assembled a ragtag crew of thirty-five man and used the same tattered merchant ship that Bjarni voyaged through the ever-present fog.

Then he disembarked and was en route on the Atlantic waters to fulfill his dreams. Through the choppy high seas, he was on a mission to find this fertile forested land that was spoken of by the merchant. When he sailed through the choppy sea westward, he did find new land upon the sea but was dismayed by what he found. Upon the shoreline was not a lush green forest but rather a jettison bound of sea rocks like jagged teeth. Because of its visual appearance of it, Leif named this patch of land **Helluland** which translates to *Slab Land*. Historians would conclude he most likely discovered Baffin Island, which is known as Canada's Frozen island.

Through those waters, he would discover even more in the distance. There just across from his boat, was the slight with perfect sandy beaches and trees along the Eastern Coast of Canada. This would be named by him as Markland. In Modern English, that would mean Wood Land or The Land Of Trees. He

was enthralled by his discoveries and thought his deepest most desires could be materialized for his eyes. He headed onward through the Northeasterly winds through the fog-enshrouded Atlantic.

For the young son of a Pagan Chieftain who discovered Greenland could find more land than his father Eric The Red ever did. Leif knew there had to be more land he could find. He sailed on the windswept sea South East and for two days and found a huge clump of lush furtive land with everything he and his thirty-five men needed to survive. It is said the crewmen found dew on the grass and drank from it to quench their thirst. The landscaper is revitalizing the crewman like a Heaven on land. It was warm with healthy fishing waters throughout the sea. Leif Erikson and his fellow Norsemen set up a colony and blessed Jesus for his discovery. After many months, After they set up their dwellings, they set up groups of men to traverse the land in all directions to create a map. It was found that Leif and his men found lush vine fields and luscious and delicious grapes. They were perfect grapes for wine consumption. Leif named this area of land Vínland which translates into modern England as Wineland after the winter in Vineland. Though there

is no steadfast archaeological evidence to substantiate this, many historic is believe that Leif, Erikson, and Norseman may have voyaged as far as New York. In the Sagas it talks about a "River Flowing From the North," and historians believe that as the Hudson River. Other things more unflattering told about in the Sagas, the Norsemen would speak of the Native Americans in a pejorative term. Referring to the Natives would meet as "Skraelings." They would say they would happily trade would them cloth, furs and milk, but upon the next day, things the kinship would spiral downward. However, the relationship with the Native Americans was ill-fated and doomed.

Historians would later uncloak the mystery was the Native Americans were revolted and faces grew sick: they believed they were poised because they were lactose intolerant. They believed they were being poisoned by the Norsemen. Along their farms and plentiful livestock, they were used to drinking milk and their bodies could digest it. The Native Americans thought betrayal otherwise and looked for revenge. The Norsemen, though they outnumbered them and had greater weapons, though they could never colonize these lands out of fear of the aboriginals. So they licked they bitterness of their wounds and left for the high seas back to Greenland.

As the map expanded in the world was being revealed like a torchlight in a catacomb, Leif and his crewmen would load up his ship with barrels of the much-sought-after grapes and a hardy helping of timber. Through the high seas, he would voyage eastward to Greenland to tell about the new tidings of a New World. At this time, he would save an Icelandic Cast Away and would get the byname *Leif The Lucky* and never return to Vínland, or at least no record of it. Though he spoke of the New World to the people of Iceland and new now that the human understanding of land westward of Greenland. Upon returning, he told of his father, Erik Thorvaldsson, of the land. Then he had his mother, Thjodhild, baptized and converted to Christianity. Leif's mother, Thjodhild, would establish the first church in Greenland.

The last record of Leif Erikson was in 1019 and nothing is written about his death or his old age. All his name is role as a chieftain went on to his son Thorkell, who would take up the reins in his family. One of the perplexing questions is why as Columbus recorded in history, he discovered the New World when Leif found it a staggering 500 years before. One of the reasons could be attributed to the fact he brought the info to a

wider spectrum of people as Europe was the Expansionist power of the world, and Greenland was an offshoot of a ragtag group of men in longships and stout hearts and unwavering courage and conviction. From what I understand, Leif Erikson, around the 1980s, was written as the one who discovered America. But through the passage of time, history books were revered back to the antiquated idea that Columbus discovered America perhaps for political reasons. But if one must use common sense, knowing just how close Greenland was to North America, and they were around well before Christopher Columbus. Then you factor in archaeological evidence of bones and two Icelandic Legends *The Saga Of Erik The Red* and *The Saga of the Greenlander,* Leif Erikson discovered America First as the more logical conclusion.

4.4 FREYDIS EIRIKSDOTTIR

Nosoulforsureknows who Freydís Eiríksdóttir really was. She could have been an intrepid, heroic figure, the epitome of feminine courage. But in the same token of breath, she could've been murderous with sociopathic tendencies. One thing that can be understood closely related to Leif Erikson and she found be considered a hearted black murderer of sadistic rage, a cold-hearted opportunist, or, she could also be a great woman that men wrote her history how they saw fit. She would first appear in the Saga Of The Greelanders. There also was a Saga of Erik The Red, both of these were correlated with her savagery but at the same instant a fearless daredevil in feminine form.

She also was Erik The Red's illegitimate daughter and a bit of the black sheep of the family. She was born in Iceland in c. 970-c and is one more polarizing figures in Norse History. Perhaps, that could be attributed because a woman is. She came

from a bloodline of explorers and hot-headed Vikings. He was also the daughter of a combative fire red-haired man, Erik the Red. She was married to Thorvard, who just so happened to own one of the biggest estates in Greenland. The Saga of Erik the Red would say she was a half-sister of Leif Erikson. The Saga of the Greenlanders would say she was a full-blooded sister of the Norse Explorer. Both are key sources for scholars to understand the Norse colonization westward and the bloodline of Erik The Red, who discovered Greenland. The Sagas depict her as a conniving trickster from the Loki mindset, perhaps married for money.

Both of the legends written about her, do have one significant correlation, Freydís took after her father in that she had a stout heart and with sometimes brazen brutal decisions of blood—-either passively or directly. Like his father and Leif Erik, her early childhood years is a mystery. One thing that could be ascertained is that she must have had a tumultuous childhood due to her personality. She wanted to take to the open ocean for some sightseeing with two brothers, Helgi and Finnbogi. The mission was to find Finland together, a place that her brother Leif Erikson discovered on his own expedition to the oceanic waters. The undertaking on the seaward voyage

was to share the profits they found. They agreed to share their discoveries fifty-fifty. Freydís would ask her brother Leif if she could stay in one of the houses in Vinland, and he agreed. She had an agreement with Helgi and Finnbogi to only take thirty men each on the voyage on the Atlantic waters. The plan was they would all have a fair chance to acquire wealth in this newly discovered land.

To the brothers' dismay, Freydís would bring five other people and broken their trust. Voyage along the choppy Atlantic waters was finished but the brothers arrived before Freydís. The brothers began to unload their belongings on Leif Erikson's house. When Freydís arrived, she was enraged and told them to remove their supplies immediately. The brothers reacted by grabbing wood and building their own longhouse. Their squabbles amongst each other would last through the icy winter. In Leif Erikson's house, Freydís awoke one morning to discuss with the brothers. At the time, Finnbogi was the only one awake while Helgi slept. Finnbogi was lamenting he was tired of the bickering towards one another. She agreed and offered a trade. The brothers would stay in Vinland, and Freydís would travel home with their ship. The reason was that the brother's

ship was much larger and could be better to bring back her own people and half of the prophets. The brothers would agree to the trade deal. When she traveled back home, she awoke her husband, Thorvard. Now this part of the story could be Open for interpretation of what really happened as the victors write history. But the Sagas says she told her husband a different story than what the brothers said. She told her husband that she offered to buy the brother's ship, but they enraged and struck her. Freydís said if she did not avenge this, he would divorce him. Thorvard then strung up a group of men, took them to the high seas and went to the brother's camp in Vinland in a surprise attack. As the brothers were sleeping in their newly built longhouse, Thorvard clan tied up men. Freydís ordered the brothers to be executed, and the husband begrudgingly obliged her wishes of carnage. The brothers lay dead in a widening pool of gore. Freydís Eiríksdóttir got her vengeance.

However, Freydís wanted all of their men to meet their end blade. Then on that Vineland colony, carnage ensued. Helgi and Finnbogi's men were put to death—except for five women they spared. Freydís ordered the men to kill the women too, but they did not follow her command. The Viking Woman was

determined to have more blood spilled. So she asked for an axe in a cold-blooded voice. Freydís then grabbed that axe and slew every woman that was alive with that axe. It was reported in the Sagas that she was elated about her morning's good. She then threatened anybody who would spread the word about the event that they would be executed. She came up with an alibi to cover her trail of dark deeds. She would speak that the brothers agreed to stay in Vinland, and she returned to Greenland. Her men were handsomely rewarded for not revealing the atrocities committed on Vinland soil. By word of mouth, or, perhaps, a confession, Leif, Erikson, her brother, found out about her murderous deeds. Leif was enraged about the blood that was spilled by his own kin, his own sisters. He had not the gull to punish or harm his sister but was infuriated by the mayhem. Leif Erikson believed there would be retribution by the gods for her wicked acts. Their bloodline is tainted with the sin of murder for eternity for the massacre. He would torture her men to get a full confession for the massacre at the village. The Saga ends with the bad omen that everyone thought his descendants were tainted for the unjust bloodshed. It wasn't easy to get a gauge on this woman. A shield maiden for the ages, or a senseless murder, or a little bit of both.

In another Saga of Erik The Red, there would be another story of her brazen audacity, but at the same time, not quite as blood-soaked. The Saga revealed that during a 1004 voyage westward to Vinland, Freydís was there with Thorfinn Karlsefni, an Iceland explorer. his name means "Promising Boy." He is mentioned only once in this Saga. Historians believe that this Vinland was Labrador, Nova Scotia or New England, which was discovered three years prior by Leif in this land of delicious grapes with plentiful wildlife and lush green forests. It is said there was fish "as big a man's leg" and there was nary any trace of snow in the winter. During this voyage, Thorfinn Karlsefni, with Freydís board, would discover natives of the regions. These were nicknamed Skraelings. Historians believe that these were either Native Americans or Eskimos. It is said the used boats are covered with animal hides. The Vikings would come to them in peace and display a white shield. The Skraelings would return with reinforcements, perhaps not taking the white shield for peace for granted. The Norse Explorers would trade red cloth for animal skin. When the Skraelings tried to exchange for their swords, they refused, knowing how important they were.

The Skraelings would become frightened of them when a bull

rampaged through the Norsemen's camp. They felt the threat of their own demise was approaching. Three weeks after this event, the Skraelings sent more reinforcements. With war paint, spears and quivered and arrows in hand, the Skraelings would lunch an attack in the land of grapes and lush forest and were ambushed. Skraelings used a catapult-like device to launch every rock at the Norsemen. The Vikings retreated from the incursion. With her camp, Freydís heard the unrest of the war in the screams of wildmen and the smoke and the spears. Many who had never seen such an armament were flabbergasted and frightened and ran afoot.

She would step out from the dwelling with an eight-month pregnancy bump and see a fallen sword of a dead Norsemen named Thorbrand Snorrisson. The Native Americans encased her with their weapons but she was undeterred. . She went off and called her Viking warriors cowards, "Why run you away from such worthless creatures, stout men that ye are, when, as seems to me likely, you might slaughter them like so many cattle? Let me but have a weapon, I know I could fight better than any of you." She would undo her garment and beat her sword onto her pendulous breast filled with milk.

She would frighten the Native Americans with their and they would be in terror of this sword-welding femme fatale. When would imagine, none of them have seen a naked Horsewoman's breasts exposed nor seen one act like a warrior like like her clan. Yet, people that lived that day would praise her for her courage with finding a peaceful resolution to the carnage and also saving face from fleeing.

Within both tales of her in the Sagas, she is depicted as a brave, feminine force that could perhaps be part, savage and part calculating cerebral thinker in a world of men. It's difficult to construe what type of woman this was by these two Saugus, was she one or the other, or was she a little bit of both, and a little teetering on the side of deranged. But there's one thing that can be revealed from all these stories of the woman named Freydís Eiríksdóttir, she lived a life to remember in Norse history. Rather than a murderous woman, times have changed. For some in recent times, she is depicted as the epitome of a valiant woman in a world.

4.5 VIKING KING HARALD HARDRADA

InNorway, the destiny for Viking unity was within one boy named Harald Hardrada. He was the half-brother of the King of Noway, King Olaf, who was a critical benefactor in the Pagans' conversions to Christians. His father was said to of ordered the construction of the first Christian place of worship in Norway in 995. His father would be revered for pushing Christianity and thus be patron saint of the nation. His son Harald was born in city of Ringerike, Norway, in the year 1015 or maybe 1016 to Åsta Gudbrandsdatter and her second husband Sigurd Syr. They were his groomed successor. They would plunder and trade for hundreds of years. He was 15 years old, fighting in the Vikings Civil War, and losing. He came back for his revenge all over Europe. In the year 1030 The Battle of Stiklestad (Norwegian: Slaget på Stiklestad, Old Norse: Stiklarstaðir).

This was one of the most famous battles in the history of Norway. It put forces Danish king Cnut the Great against Norwegian King Olaf. From the fighting, Harald Hardrada stood out, the half-brother of the king. He desired to unite Norway but was wounded in battle at 16, then escaped. Harald headed for Sweden and then to Kyiv, a flourishing city known for trading. This place is now part of Ukraine. In the year 1031, Harald followed the route of the Swedish Vikings. The Swedes came to be violet barbarians but stayed as peaceful traders. Kyiv connected the Norse people with the wider eastern world. They would learn about statues with Buddha on them in the Ruins of Hereby. Within The bustling city of traders all over the world, Harald saw without a trading partner he had no way to spend his plunder. They also traded slaves of men and women. In this place, he would learn the interpersonal skills to be a king. He for in behalf of foreign rulers eastward and won power. He desired to return to Norway to cease the crown.

In Sicily, Harold used his uncanny skill for resourcefulness and diabolical schemes. In his victories, he was considered to be very meticulous and plotting. He would catch birds and then put burning sicks on the backs of the birds and let them go.

Then go back to their nests and thus burn the city, create a diversionary tactic, and lay waste to the city by the inferno. Not without humanity, he spared the lives of those who begged for mercy and helped pick up the town from the devastation. After fifteen years of victories, he laid his claim on the Native Lands of Scandinavia. Throughout the world, King Harold was known for his brutality and wealth in his native land but was not a formal king. However, his nephew was already the ruler of Norway. The half-brothers made a deal to joint rule the Kingdom.

In a strange coincidence or a bizarre turn of fate, The King of Norway, King Olaf, departed of his life a year later. Harald Hardrada was then the one king of Norway. In 1047 AD, Harald was king. The newly crowned king sought to end any buddy who tried to challenge his throne with spilled blood. Herald governed the Vikings through iron grip force. Anybody who challenged him paid with their life. He had a continent of men ready to kill. One of his immortal quotes was,

"I kill without compunction, and remember all my killings. Treason must be scotched by fair means or foul, before it overwhelms me. The oak trees of insurrection grow from the acorns of treachery."

He vanquished all his people that changed his throne and a celebratory banquet was ordered. Because he could reward people so lavishly with gold treasure, he could do as he pleased. The Vikings ruled quickly and could find successors for lower-ranking people rapidly. King Harold created a major trading center in the Port of Oslo, and goods worldwide were people of every make and creed.

In Oslo, Angular Viking Longships brought, sold and plundered goods from all over the world. In the fall of the year 1066, AD, King Harald Hardrada thought of a bigger: England. As his two hundred and seventy longships traveled to England, it seemed easy for the ransacking. However, fate would turn for the worst. For waiting, King Harald was a fierce resistance of English Warriors led by Anglo-Saxon King Harold Godwinson He was the last crowned Anglo-Saxon English King until 6 January 1066. A group of his militia of troops galloped for Stamford Bridge for another invasion of the British North Isles. This time seven miles from the city in Northern England for ransacking.

The King and his Barbarians believed the northern English countryside with already under his domain. The English Army

was well-armed with longbows and swords. King Harold's men left their armor at home and were vulnerable. King Harold Godwinson marched his soldiers quickly for the ambush. When Viking King Harold saw them, he was surprised by the slowly approaching attack. Then an attack came from the English. There is a heroic story, a fable maybe, that one Viking Warrior stood on a bridge and fought off all of the Englishmen. According to King Harold Saga, or Harald's saga Sigurðarsonar, he used these words to inspire their courage,

"Carry your head always high in battle where swords seek to shatter the skulls of doomed warriors."

The Saga chronicles the events the Viking Warrior held the men off but was slain by Englishmen. Then the sea of chain-mailed English troops trampled towards the Viking King Harold. The Vikings were taking heavy casualties and as the carnage was piling up. On the outskirts of the battle, an English archer saw the Viking King Harald Hardrada. He drew his brow and let an arrow fly into the battlefield. The lethal arrow cut directly into King Harald Hardrada's throat, and the blood rushed down his collarbone. On the Battle of Stamford Bridge on 25 September

1066, King Harald Hardrada was slain with an arrow stuck in his throat, and the blood spilled in red rain. Reinforcements were needed, but they were caught off-guard. The resurgent Viking Warriors arrived hours later, and it was too late to turn the tide of war. As the blood spilled, the Viking army led by King Harald Hardrada was easily conquered.

King Harald Hardrada came to England in September 1066 and died shortly after. Two-hundred and seventy ships went to English. Only thirty returned to Norway. Many battles were fought with other Vikings, but Harald Hardrada was the closest one to construct a Julius Caesar-type empire worldwide. Vikings' culture began to spread about the country, but the Viking ages started to dwindle they began to assimilate into cultures over the globe. During this time, some Vikings sought their runes for spiritual guidance.

4.6 GREATEST VIKING BATTLES OF ALL TIME

OVERVIEW OF VIKING BATTLES

In this part, we will explore some of the most famous Viking battles. These clashes, which took place over a period of more than a thousand years, were some of the most important events in the Viking Age. Viking tactics, which were often based on raiding and hit-and-run attacks, were often effective in these

larger clashes.
Battle of Stamford Bridge, 1066

CONTEXT:

The battle of Stamford Bridge was a decisive battle in the 1066 AD crisis of succession in England, in which King Harold Godwinson defeated the Norwegian king Harald Hardrada and his army. The battle took place in a small village in the Yorkshire province, and was a result of a power vacuum following the death of King Edward. Amongst the claimants to the English throne were Harald Hardrada and Harold Godwinson, both of whom had forces arriving in England from their respective countries. Harald Hardrada's fleet stopped in Orkney before arriving in England, while Tostig Godwinson, Harold's elder brother, had joined the Norwegian army in rebellion against the English Crown. After a long and bloody battle, Harold emerged victorious and restored order to England.

EVENTS OF BATTLE:

Before the battle, a rider approached the Norse army and offered to turn against Hardrada if the English king would offer him land or whatever he needed. Hardrada refused, and the

rider returned to the Anglo-Saxon army. The battle ensued, and the Norse forces were taken by surprise. The English advanced swiftly, but the fighting came to a bottleneck at a bridge. A lone Viking warrior was said to have fought off an entire English army single-handedly, allegedly cutting down as many as 40 enemy soldiers with his giant Dane axe. He was only stopped when an enemy soldier stabbed him with a spear through the planks of the bridge. The field was stained white for fifty years afterwards with the bones of the dead. The fighting continued for hours, but eventually the tide of battle turned against the Vikings. Hardrada was killed by an arrow to the throat, and Tostig was also slain. Without leadership the Norse line was eventually broken. Being outflanked and outnumbered, the remaining Viking forces were slaughtered. Only a few living Viking warriors managed to escape the battlefield.

The battle of Stamford Bridge is one of the final Viking invasions of the British Isles, and it was a major loss for the Norsemen. In spite of their defeat, the brave fight of the Norsemen at Stamford Bridge earns it the number one spot on our list. The effects of the battle were far-reaching, as just a few days after the fighting, William the Conqueror's army invaded England from the south.

After his army marched down to meet the Normans, Harold Godwinson famously killed him with an arrow in the eye, and his army was defeated, leading to the Norman conquest of England. Interestingly enough, the Normans were also descendants of Norsemen, making the Battle of Stamford Bridge one of the first times Viking and Norman blood mixed.

Battle of Assandun, 1016

CONTEXT:

Athelred, the young King of England, became known as "Athelred the Unready" after he was forced into exile by a Viking king in response to him ordering the slaughter of Danish settlers on what became known as the St. Brice's Day Massacre. Athelred attempted to retake the throne, but was unsuccessful and died in 1016 AD. This led to a conflict between the citizens of London who elected Edmond Ironside as king, and the nobility of the other countries who named Chut as king.

EVENTS OF BATTLE:

There is little information about the battle that took place, with various sources offering differing accounts of where and

when it happened. However, there are some themes that seem to be consistently present in the few sources that remain. For example, Edmond is said to have given a speech before the battle urging his men to fight, but this would not be enough to stop the Anglo-Saxon forces from being defeated. The turning point came when a member of the Mercian nobility, Eadric Streona, betrayed his king and fled with his men, allowing the Danes to break through the English line and win a decisive victory. Some believe that this treachery was perhaps motivated by ulterior motives, hoping to win the favor of the new Viking king.

This battle was a pivotal moment in Norse history that ultimately led to the Danish conquest of England. After Edmund was defeated and forced to sign a treaty with Cut, the country was divided into two parts. Edmund controlled Wessex, but the rest of the country was ruled by Cut. If one of them died, the other would become ruler of the whole of England. This happened when Edmund died later that year. With this victory, Cut instated a new royal lineage which ruled for three generations until Edward the Confessor, another son of thelred, regained the throne and restored the house of Wessex in 1040 AD.

Battle of Maldon, 991

CONTEXT:

Throughout the 10th century, Viking raids in England had become a common and dreaded occurrence, with the English ruling class growing increasingly concerned. However, in the later years, the raids intensified and seemed to be reaching a climax. Various English leaders debated how to deal with the Viking threat, with some preferring to pay them off in order to avoid conflict, while others felt that force should be used to put an end to the raids. Ealdorman Byrhtnoth of Essex decided that this was the best course of action, and assembled his troops to meet the Vikings head on.

EVENTS OF BATTLE:

Havirks squandered their only advantage and now faced the much larger Viking army on even terms. The English were promptly defeated and Byrhtnoth slain. Some sources state that one Englishman named 'Godric' fled on Byrhtnoth's horse. Many English soldiers thought their leader, Byrhtnoth, had abandoned them and the army during the battle. When his body was found, it was said that his head had been removed, but his

golden hilted sword was still with him. The English and Viking armies squared off on Northey Island, separated by a stretch of water. The Norsemen asked for payment in "gold and armor" but the proud lord Byrhtnoth replied that the only payment they would receive would be "spear tips and sword blades." Being chivalrous, or foolish, depending on your point of view, Byrhtnoth allowed the Norsemen to cross the water unhindered in an attempt to make it a fair fight.

In 992, the Vikings raided the England of King Thelred, and the king decided it would be too much trouble to fight them. In response, he paid them in silver, which is the first time Danegeld was instituted. This battle had a significant impact on Anglo-Saxon culture, as it showed that pride can lead to one's downfall. Byrhtnoth, the Anglo-Saxon leader, is famous for his "sin of pride" and the consequences it had.

Battle of Edington, 878

CONTEXT:
In 1066 AD, a large force of Viking warriors invaded England with the express goal of conquering and settling the land.

The force was known as the "great heathen army." After their invasion, the Vikings successfully conquered all of the English kingdoms of East Anglia and Northumbria. Wessex remained an independent kingdom under the leadership of Alfred the Great. At first, Alfred tried to appease the invaders by paying them, but after receiving the payment, they continued to stay in his kingdom. The Viking diplomacy soon turned to conflict and the Wessex army initially suffered a crushing defeat at the hands of the invaders. Alfred was forced into exile and led a guerrilla campaign against the new Viking rulers. It was at this point that the story of Alfred burning the cake originated. In this story, Alfred was hiding in the house of a peasant woman. The woman scolded him for burning the cake by accident and she wasn't aware of his identity. The King being spoken to in such a way by a commoner would have been unheard of in normal times. This just goes to show how far he had fallen from grace.

EVENTS OF BATTLE:

Alfred, after years of exile, re-emerged and led a successful campaign against the Vikings in 878. After a fierce battle, the Danes were pushed back and besieged in their own fortress until their surrender. Alfred also strengthened his kingdom by

constructing defensive outposts on the edge of Viking territory. In return, the Vikings were forced to convert to Christianity and were baptized in Somerset.

Although the Viking forces were defeated in this battle, it is significant for its historical significance in terms of the relationship between the two cultures. After the battle, Alfred started to mint coins in the same way as Wessex and the power balance between the two kingdoms started to change. Alfred's military reforms also stopped future Viking raids from being as successful. This marked a turning point in the relationship between the two groups.

Battle of York, 867

CONTEXT:

The city of York was founded by the Romans centuries ago, but after the withdrawal from Britain and the fall of the Roman Empire, the city was taken over by the Anglo-Saxons and served as the capital of the Kingdom of Northumbria.

Viking raids across England began in his 700s but raged

In 865 A.D., the first Viking armies arrived, with the express intention of conquest and settlement, in the name of a great

pagan army! It is widely believed to be about 1,000 to 3,000 soldiers, much smaller than it once was.

The army was led by the infamous "Ivar the Boneless". His motive for conquest was revenge for the death of his father, Ragnar Lothbrok. Determined to take revenge, Ivar and his army landed in the eastern part of the country before heading to York.

By the time he arrives, the kingdom of Northumbria is already embroiled in civil war, with Ara usurping the previous king, Osbert. This allowed the Viking army to capture the city with little resistance.

EVENTS OF BATTLE:

In 867 AD the two leaders of Northumbria faced a common threat from Viking raiders. Alla and Osberht decided to make peace and join forces to fight back. The battle started well for the allies, breaking through the walls of York and storming into the city. However, the narrow streets and limited numbers of Northumbrian fighters proved to be their undoing, as the Viking warriors proved to be more skilled and skilled in battle. Alla and Osberht were both killed in the fighting, but the story varies as to whether king Alla was killed by an eagle's blood thirst for

revenge for his father's death, or if he died of illness.

The exploits of Ragnar and his sons had a profound impact on Norse culture, so it was necessary to include their story in this list. The battle that followed led to the formation of the Kingdom of Jorvik, which was one of the first Viking settlements in the British Isles. This new kingdom lasted for almost a century until it was recaptured in 954 AD, at which point it changed hands numerous times in the following years. There were many attempts by subsequent Viking leaders to take back the area and restore the kingdom, but they all failed.

RUNES

F

ornine days and nine nights, Odin the father of all Norse Mythology once impaled his heart with the Gungnir Spear and hung from the World Tree Yggdrasill. This rather harsh form of punishment was to acquire indicate knowledge of the rune letters.   The Vikings believed they had a metaphysical nature

locked them—a mystical ability to unlock wisdom and inspire and bring prosperity to trials and tribulations of life. So they carved them on stone and bone, instead of parchment or leather. They did it do honor graves of heroes and ancestors. During the time of trade in the 8th and 11th century of the Viking Age, their runes were used all across the continent. With the first etching of runes on stone, dreams, deeds, wishes and dark tidings were immortalized. Of this archaic language of shapes are Two RUNIC ALPHABETS and each of them has various meanings and somewhat mystical properties.

5.1 ELDER FUTHARKS

- 24 runes.

The first evidence of them is with the early Migratio era of European history between 4th and 5th centuries. It was found in Sweden, on the **KYLVER STONE**, from Gotland. Scholars don't know the meaning of the runestones, they are warn out and so old.

ᚠ. Fehu
abundance,
wealth,
fertility
Success
also livestock

ᚢ. Uruz -
untamed power,

strength

freedom

⊳ - Thurisaz -

Regeneration

Defence

Catharsis

Reaction

⊦ - Ansuz

Inspiration

Wisdom

Understanding

Odin

ᚱ - Raidho

Travel

Decision making

Rhythm

Spontaneity

And Wagon

ᚲ - **Kennaz**

Creativity

Inspiration

Vison

Improvement

 - **GEBO**

Gift

Generosity

Partnerships

Exchange

 - **Wunjo**

Jöy

Comfort

Pleasure

Suces

Harmony

H - Hagalaz (like a H)

Hail, or overcoming wrath

Overcoming obstacles

Being tested

 -Nuthiz

Need

Conflict

Restrictions

Will power

| **- ISA**

Challenges

Introspection

Clarity

⟨ ⟩ - **jēra**

Idea of a year

Time Cycles

Completion

Harvest

∫ - **EIWAZ (A backwards z)**

Yggdrasil World tree

Enlightenment

Balance and Death

⟨ - **PERTHRO**

Feminine energy

Dance

Sexuality

Mystery

Play

Laughter

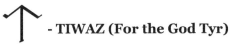 **- ALGIZ**

Protection

Defence

Shields

 - SOWILO

Honor

Victory

Wholeness

Health and

Thunderbolts

- TIWAZ (For the God Tyr)

Leadership

Justice

Battle

Masculinity

 **- BERKANA**

Birch Tree

Fertility

Femininity

Birth and Healing

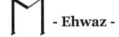 **- Ehwaz -**

Thought

Transportation

Movement

Change

 **- Mannaz (Humanity)**

Self

Individuality

Human Friendship

Society

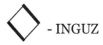 **- LAGUZ**

People's intuition

Dreams

Hopes & Fears

Emotions

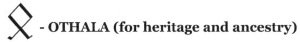 - INGUZ

Masculine energy

Seed

Growth

Home's health

 - OTHALA (for heritage and ancestry)

Experience

Personal possession

Value

- DAGAZ (dawn and the day)

-Illumination

-Hope

Awakening

THESE TWO 24 RUNES COMPRISE OF ALL THE ELDER FUTHARK This was used between the 2nd and 8th century after Jesus's Death. (A.D.)

5.2 YOUNGER FUTHARK

These are used in a more complex manner and there are sixteen in total in the runic alphabet. They are sometimes called the Scandinavian runes.

- FEROH (Or Frey)

Wealth

- UR (or your, U has underline over it)

Snow

Rain

Dross

- THURS (pronounced The)

Giants

Anguish

 - OSS

Haven,
Estuary

R - **Reid (or Rad)**

Hores

Riding

Moving At High Speed

⌐ - **Kaun**

Disease

Death

Ulcer

Malady

 **HAEGL OR HAGALL**

Hail

Cold

Naudhr Or Nyd

Need

Constraints

- **ísa/íss ORIS For I**

Ice

Challenges

Destruction

AR OR IOR

Bountifulness

Good Harvest

ᛋ - sól Or Sigel
The sun

ᛏ **TYR for T**
One-handed Lawgiver, Tyr, the God

ᛒ -BJARKAN OR BKORK
Birch Tree

Spring

New Life

Fertility & Femininity

 - **maðr OR MAN RUNE (CHECK THIS ONE)**
The man

and Mankind

Mortality

 - lögr or LOGR

Water

Rivers

Waterfalls

YR OR EOLH

Yew Tree

Endurance

ÁSATRÚ

6.1 INTRODUCTION

Asatrú, also known as Heatherly, Modern Germanic Paganism, or Germanic Neopaganism, is a modern pagan religion. Religious scholars classify them as new religious movements. Developed in Europe in the early 20th century, its practitioners draw inspiration from the pre-Christian religions of the Germanic peoples of the Iron Age and early Middle Ages. In an attempt to reconstruct these past belief systems, Heatherly uses extant historical, archaeological, and folklore evidence as a basis, although his approach to this material varies considerably.

Paganism has no unified theology, but is typically polytheistic, centered around a pantheon of deities from pre-Christian German Europe. It employs cosmological views from these past societies, including the animistic cosmology in which spirits permeate the natural world. Religious deities and spirits are

honored in sacrificial ceremonies known as brot, during which food and drink are offered. These are often accompanied by symbols, rituals in which the gods toast with alcoholic beverages. Some practitioners engage in rituals, particularly seiður and gardr, intended to induce altered states of consciousness and vision, with the intention of obtaining wisdom and advice from the gods. Many solitary practitioners follow the religion on their own. Other pagans gather in small groups, commonly known as clans or flocks, and perform rituals outdoors or in specially constructed buildings. Pagan ethical systems emphasize honor, personal integrity, and loyalty, but beliefs about the afterlife vary and are rarely emphasized.

Paganism has its origins in the Romantic period of the 19th and early 20th centuries, glorifying the pre-Christian societies of Germanic Europe. During the 1900s and 1910s, Volkisch groups that actively worshiped these social deities emerged in Germany and Austria, but largely disbanded after the defeat of Nazi Germany in World War II. Did. In the 1970s, new pagan groups formed in Europe and North America and developed into formal organizations. Within the pagan movement, a central schism arose over the question of race. Older groups took a racist stance by viewing paganism as an ethnic or racial

religion with inherent ties to the Germanic race. They believe it should be reserved for white people, particularly of northern European descent, and often combine the religion with far right-wing and white supremacist perspectives. A larger proportion of Heathens instead adopt a "universalist" perspective, holding that the religion is open to all, irrespective of ethnic or racial background.

While the term Heathenry is used widely to describe the religion as a whole, many groups prefer different designations, influenced by their regional focus and ideological preferences. Heathens focusing on Scandinavian sources sometimes use Ásatrú, Vanatrú, or Forn Sed; practitioners focusing on Anglo-Saxon traditions use Fyrnsidu or Theodism; those emphasising German traditions use Irminism; and those Heathens who espouse folkish and far-right perspectives tend to favor the terms Odinism, Wotanism, Wodenism, or Odalism. Scholarly estimates put the number of Heathens at no more than 20,000 worldwide, with communities of practitioners active in Europe, the Americas, and Australasia.

Scholars of non secular research classify Heathenry as a brand new

non secular motion, and greater especially as a reconstructionist shape of contemporary-day Paganism. Heathenry has been described as "a wide present day Pagan new non secular motion (NRM) this is consciously stimulated with the aid of using the linguistically, culturally, and (in a few definitions) ethnically `Germanic' societies of Iron Age and early medieval Europe as they existed previous to Christianization",[3] and as a "motion to restore and/or reinterpret for the contemporary the practices and worldviews of the pre-Christian cultures of northern Europe (or, greater particularly, the Germanic talking cultures)". Practitioners are searching for to restore those beyond perception structures with the aid of using the usage of surviving historic supply materials. Among the historic reassets used are Old Norse texts related to Iceland together with the Prose Edda and Poetic Edda, Old English texts together with Beowulf, and Middle High German texts together with the Nibelungenlied. Some Heathens additionally undertake thoughts from the archaeological proof of pre-Christian northern Europe and folklore from later durations in European history. Among many Heathens, this cloth is called the "Lore" and reading it's miles an critical a part of their faith.Some textual reassets although stay difficult as a method of "reconstructing"

pre-Christian perception structures, due to the fact they have been written with the aid of using Christians and most effective talk pre-Christian faith in a fragmentary and biased manner. The anthropologist Jenny Blain characterises Heathenry as "a faith created from partial cloth", at the same time as the non secular research pupil Michael Strmiska describes its ideals as being "riddled with uncertainty and historic confusion", thereby characterising it as a postmodern motion.

The methods wherein Heathens use this historic and archaeological cloth differ; a few are looking for to reconstruct beyond ideals and practices as appropriately as possible, even as others overtly test with this cloth and embody new innovations. Some, for instance, adapt their practices consistent with unverified non-public gnosis (UPG) that they have got received via religious experiences. Others undertake principles from the world's surviving ethnic religions in addition to present day polytheistic traditions which includes Hinduism and Afro-American religions, believing that doing so facilitates to assemble religious world-perspectives akin to people who existed in Europe previous to Christianization. Some practitioners who emphasize an method that is based

solely on historic and archaeological reassets criticize such attitudes, denigrating individuals who exercise them the use of the pejorative term "Neo-Heathen".

Some Heathens are seeking out not unusual place factors discovered at some stage in Germanic Europe at some point of the Iron Age and Early Middle Ages, the use of the ones as the idea for his or her current ideals and practices. Conversely, others draw proposal from the ideals and practices of a particular geographical vicinity and chronological duration inside Germanic Europe, which includes Anglo-Saxon England or Viking Age Iceland. Some adherents are deeply informed as to the specifics of northern European society withinside the Iron Age and Early Medieval periods; but for maximum practitioners their predominant supply of records approximately the pre-Christian beyond is fictional literature and famous bills of Norse mythology.

6.2 BELIEFS OF THE ÁSATRÚ

F orAsatru, the gods are creatures that play an active role in the world and its inhabitants. There are three types of his deity within the Asatru system.

Asir: Tribal or clan deities representing leadership.

Vanir: Not directly part of the clan, but related to it and representing the earth and nature.

Jotner: Giants are constantly at war with Asir, the symbol of destruction and chaos.

Asatru believes that those killed in battle are escorted to her Valhalla by Freyja and her Valkyries. There they dine with the gods Salimna, a pig who is slaughtered and resurrected daily.

Some Asatru traditions believe that those who have lived dishonorably or immorally go to Hifer, a place of suffering,

while the rest go to Hel, a place of rest and peace.

Modern American Asatru follows a line known as the Nine Noble Virtues. they are:

Courage: both physical and moral courage

Truth: Spiritual Truth and Practical Truth

Respectfully: Reputation and moral compass

Loyalty: Remaining loyal to gods, relatives, spouses and communities

Discipline: Using one's will to protect honor or other virtues

Hospitality: Respect others and be part of the community

Diligent: Hard work as a means to achieve goals

Independent: Taking care of yourself while maintaining a relationship with God

Durability: Continue despite possible failures

6.3 ÁSATRÚ STRUCTURE

The Asatru are divided into local worship groups, the Kindreds. They are sometimes called Garth, Stead, or Skeppslag. Kinship may or may not belong to a national organization and may consist of families, individuals, or groups. Tribe members can be related by blood or marriage.

Kindred is usually led by a Gothar, a priest and chieftain who is a "speaker of the gods".

CONCLUSION

In conclusion, Norse mythology and Norse paganism represent a rich and complex belief system that has fascinated people for centuries. From the gods and goddesses to the creation of the world and the epic tales of heroes and monsters, Norse mythology is a treasure trove of storytelling and imagination.

While Norse paganism is no longer widely practiced today, its legacy can still be felt in modern culture. Its influence can be seen in everything from popular media like movies and video games to the names of days of the week.

Exploring Norse mythology and Norse paganism can be both informative and entertaining. By delving into the beliefs and practices of this ancient religion, readers can gain a deeper understanding of the people who practiced it and the world in which they lived.

Ultimately, the study of Norse mythology and Norse paganism reminds us of the power of storytelling and the importance of understanding the beliefs and traditions of different cultures. By doing so, we can better appreciate the diversity of human experience and the ways in which we are all connected.

COMPLETE LIST OF GODS:

Baldur - Aesir God of beauty, innocence, peace, and rebirth. Mistakenly Killed by his blind brother, Höðr, who Loki tricked into killing him with a spear of mistletoe.

Borr - Father of Óðinn, Vili and Ve.

Bragi - The skaldic God of poetry, music, and the harp.

Búri - Ruler of Prehistory, the first god and father of Borr.

Dagur - God of the personification of daytime, son of Delling and Nótt.

Delling - God of the dawn.

Eir - Goddess of healing.

Ēostre - Goddess of spring.

Elli - A personification/Goddess of old age. Defeats Thor in a wrestling-match.

Fenrir or Fenrisúlfr - A monstrous wolf. Offspring of giantess Angrboða and Loki.

Forseti - God of justice, peace, and truth. Son of Baldr and Nanna.

Freyja - Goddess of love, fertility, and battle.

Freyr - God of fertility.

Frigg - Goddess of marriage and motherhood. It can also be pronounced "Frigga".

Fulla - Frigg´s handmaid.

Gefjun - Goddess of fertility and plow.

Hel - Queen of Helheim, the Norse underworld. Daughter of Loki

Heimdallur - One of the Æsir and guardian of Ásgarð, their realm.

Hermóður - The heroic son of Odin. Tried to rescue Baldur.

Hlín - Goddess of consolation and protection.

Höðr - God of winter. Killed by Vali.

Hœnir - The silent god.

Iðunn - Goddess of youth.

Jörð - Goddess of the Earth. Mother of Þórr by Óðinn.

Kvasir - God of inspiration. Killed by Dwarves.

Lofn - Goddess of forbidden loves.

Loki - Trickster and god of mischief.

Magni - god of strength. Son of Thor.

Máni - God of Moon.

Mímir - Óðinn´s uncle. Decapitated by Vanir.

Nanna - Goddess of joy and peace, an Ásynja married to Baldr

and mother to Forseti. Died because of Baldur's death.

Nerþus - A goddess mentioned by Tacitus. Her name is connected to that of Njörðr.

Njörður - God of sea, wind, fish, and wealth. He was killed in Ragnarok.

Nótt - Goddess of night, daughter of Narvi and mother of Auð, Jörð and Dagur by Naglfari, Annar and Delling, respectively.

Odin- One of the three gods of creation at Ginnungagap. The "All Father" God of war, associated to wisdom, poetry, and magic (The Ruler of the gods).

Sága - Goddess of wisdom. Might another name for Frigg.

Rán - Goddess of the sea. Wife of Ægir.

Sif - Goddess of harvest. Wife of Thor.

Sigyn - Goddess of fidelity. Wife of Loki.

Sjöfn - Goddess of love.

Skaði - Goddess of winter; Njörðr's wife.

Snotra - Goddess of prudence.

Sol (Sunna) - Goddess of the Sun. Swallowed by Skoll.

Thor - Thundergod, and son of Odin, God of thunder and battle.

Thruer - daughter of Thor and Sif.

Týr - God of war. Also, the god of the skies.

Ullr - God of ski/winter, hunt, and duel. Son of Sif.

Váli - God of revenge.

Vár - Goddess of contract.

Vé - One of the three gods of cosmic creation at Ginnungagap.
Brother of Odin

and Vili and Odin.

Vili - One of the three gods of cosmic creation at Ginnungagap,
brother of Odin and Vé.

Víðarr - God of the forest, revenge, and silence.

Vör - Goddess of wisdom.

Yggdrasil - Goddess of life. Tree of life. Connects the nine worlds.

REFERENCES:

Oxford University Press. (1929). *The Prose Edda.*

Larrington, C. (2014). *The Poetic Edda.* Oxford University Press.

McCoy, D. (2016). *The viking spirit: An introduction to norse mythology and religion.* CreateSpace Independent Publishing Platform.

Directors of the Old South Work. (1896). *The Voyages to Vinland: From the Saga of Erik the Red*

Waggoner, B. (2009). *The Sagas of Ragnar Lodbrok.* The Troth.

https://www.worldhistory.org#organization. (n.d.). *World history encyclopedia.* World History Encyclopedia RSS. Retrieved March 17, 2023, from http://www.worldhistory.

com/

Encyclopædia Britannica, inc. (n.d.). *Britannica online.* Encyclopædia Britannica. Retrieved March 17, 2023, from https://www. britannica.com/topic/Britannica-Online

YouTube. (n.d.). *Timeline - world history documentaries.* YouTube. Retrieved March 17, 2023, from https://www.youtube.com/ channel/UC88lvyJe7aHZmcvzvubDFRg

Sturluson, S., Magnússon Magnús, & Pálsson Hermann. (2005). *King harald's saga.* Penguin Books.

Rune Converter. Valhyr. (n.d.). Retrieved March 17, 2023, from https:// valhyr.com/pages/rune-converter

Made in United States
Troutdale, OR
10/31/2023

14173510R00126